IN THE FOOTSTEPS OF BONNIE PRINCE CHARLIE

JIMMIE MACGREGOR is a graduate of the Glasgow School of Art, and has been, among other things, a schoolteacher, engraver, potter, naturalist, labourer, hospital porter, author, illustrator, and radio and television presenter. He was deeply involved in the early days of the folk music revival in Britain, and remained in the forefront of that movement for more than twenty years, becoming a household name through countless radio, concert and television appearances. He has toured the length and breadth of Britain, and in Canada, Israel, America, Australia, Belgium, Holland, France, New Zealand, Germany, Russia, Austria and the Middle East.

Jimmie has made more than twenty long-playing albums, while several of his own songs and tunes have been used by fellow musicians, and he has composed and played theme music for radio and television. He has won an award for voice-over commentary on video, and his own highly successful daily radio programme, which is in its sixth year, was granted a special prize by the Royal Society for the Protection of Birds, for significant contribution to wildlife and conservation. Jimmie has been made Scot of the year by two separate organisations, and is honorary vice-president of the Scottish Wildlife Trust, the Glasgow branch of the Scottish Youth Hostels Association, and Scottish Conservation Projects.

The BBC television series, *In the Footsteps of Bonnie Prince Charlie*, on which this book is based, is the third in a series which includes *On the West Highland Way* and *Macgregor's Scotland – the Moray Coast, Speyside & the Cairngorms*. Another outdoor series was filmed in 1988.

IN THE FOOTSTEPS OF
BONNIE PRINCE CHARLIE

JIMMIE MACGREGOR

BBC BOOKS

By the same author

On the West Highland Way
Macgregor's Scotland: the Moray Coast, Speyside & the Cairngorms
Scottish Poetry from Macgregor's Gathering
Macgregor's Gathering of Scottish Dialect Poetry
Singing our Own pub. Holmes McDougall
Jimmie Macgregor's Folk-Songs of Scotland (Volumes I and II)
pub. Jarrolds, Norwich

Acknowledgements
My special thanks to Dr Hamish Henderson for his song
The Seven Men of Knoydart.

Picture credits
BBC HULTON PICTURE LIBRARY pages 15, 19, 65 and 86;
MANSELL COLLECTION pages 17, 38 and 41. All the
remaining photographs were supplied by
Jimmie MacGregor.

Published by BBC Books
A division of BBC Enterprises Ltd
Woodlands, 80 Wood Lane, London W12 0TT
First published 1988
Reprinted 1988
© Jimmie Macgregor 1988
ISBN 0 563 20654 3
Typeset in 10/12pt Bembo by Phoenix Photosetting, Chatham, Kent
Printed and bound in England by Mackays of Chatham PLC, Chatham, Kent
Cover printed by Fletchers, Norwich

C ONTENTS

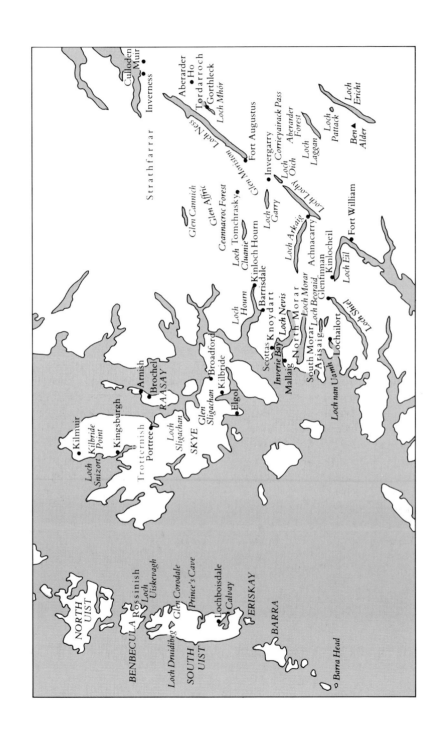

INTRODUCTION

O N 16 APRIL 1987, on the anniversary of the battle of Culloden, and one year short of the 200th anniversary of the death of Prince Charles Edward Stuart, I stood on Drummossie Moor, near Culloden, in Inverness-shire. This is the site of the last pitched battle fought on British soil. It was a conflict which threw the Highlands of Scotland into turmoil and ended for ever the aspirations of the house of Stuart to the British throne. When the defeated prince fled the field with a few followers, he faced life as a fugitive, hunted relentlessly through the hills and glens which he had come to claim as his own. After five months of extraordinary hardship and hazard, he made a miraculous escape to France.

I had decided to attempt to follow the prince's escape route, in so far as it is known; and with Dennis Dick, television producer, film-maker and station manager of BBC Aberdeen, was to televise the venture in series form. Dennis had already reconnoitred much of the route, and we decided not only to pursue the prince's adventures, but to make contact with people living and working in the area; including direct descendants of those who had been involved in the '45 and in Charles Edward's amazing escape. I was also interested in all aspects of the country through which I would be travelling, so that this book will offer some of my impressions of how the Highlands and islands have changed since *Bliadhna Tearlach* – 'Charlie's Year'.

I have also attempted to put the prince in some kind of historical perspective by briefly tracing the origins and development of the house of Stuart, whose adventures and misadventures have so enlivened the pages of history.

THE STUART AND HANOVERIAN SUCCESSION

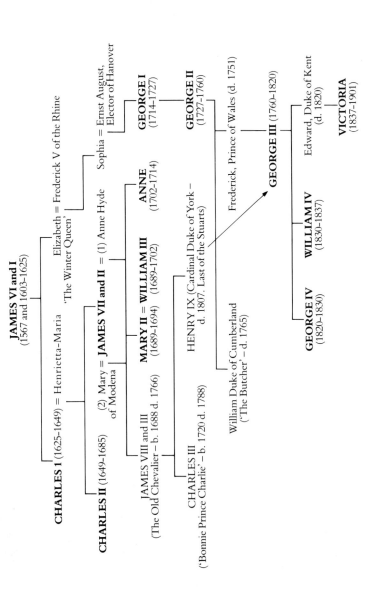

JAMES VI and I
(1567 and 1603-1625)

CHARLES 1 (1625-1649) = Henrietta-Maria   Elizabeth = Frederick V of the Rhine
'The Winter Queen'

Sophia = Ernst August,
Elector of Hanover

CHARLES II (1649-1685)

(2) Mary = **JAMES VII and II** = (1) Anne Hyde
of Modena

MARY II = WILLIAM III   **ANNE**
(1689-1694)   (1689-1702)   (1702-1714)

GEORGE I
(1714-1727)

GEORGE II
(1727-1760)

JAMES VIII and III
('The Old Chevalier' – b. 1688 d. 1766)

HENRY IX (Cardinal Duke of York –
d. 1807. Last of the Stuarts)

Frederick, Prince of Wales (d. 1751)

CHARLES III
('Bonnie Prince Charlie' – b. 1720 d. 1788)

GEORGE III (1760-1820)

William Duke of Cumberland
('The Butcher' – d. 1765)

Edward, Duke of Kent
(d. 1820)

GEORGE IV   **WILLIAM IV**
(1820-1830)   (1830-1837)

VICTORIA
(1837-1901)

FAREWELL TO A PRINCE

O N THE morning of 4 October 1956, early snow dusted the hills of Arisaig, in the West Highlands. The waters of Loch Nan Uamh were foam-flecked and broken by an icy wind from the north-west. Two hundred brave folk faced squalls of hail and sleet to gather on an exposed rocky promontory, for a ceremony which would celebrate a disaster: the failure of the '45, and the departure from Scotland, 210 years before, of Prince Charles Edward Louis John Sylvester Maria Casimir Stuart; known, to the great relief of anyone writing about him, as Bonnie Prince Charlie.

The prince's memorial cairn

The ceremony took the form of the unveiling of a cairn, and the planting of the flags which had draped it; and as the saltire of Scotland fell away, a *piobaireachd* was played. The piper was John McKinnon of Arisaig, who had built the memorial cairn. The opening ceremony was performed by the Countess of Erroll, twenty-eighth hereditary High Constable of Scotland, and a direct descendant of Lord Kilmarnock, who ended his life on Tower Hill for his part in the Jacobite rising of 1745. The countess was received by Cameron of Lochiel, descended from one of the most influential figures of the '45, and by Mr F. S. Cameron Head of Lochailart, whose ancestors were the Jacobite chieftains of Glendessary. The eminent naturalist and author Seton Gordon was also present, as well as ordinary men and women from many parts of Scotland, England and America.

Speeches were made and great music was heard. Angus McPherson, honorary piper to the '45 association, and one of an unbroken line going back to James McPherson, piper to the famous Cluny McPherson, played *My King Has Landed in Moidart*, *The Prince's Salute*, and that simple but noble lament, *Lochaber No More*. Mr Cameron Head himself provided *Prince Charlie's Farewell to Moidart*, composed at the time of the prince's flight, and held by Cameron Head's family since that time. This was the tune's first public airing for 210 years; a poignant moment. Indeed, the whole ceremony was an emotional one: but what were these people doing here? What were they celebrating? Charles Edward's attempt to regain the throne for the Stuarts had been a disastrous failure, and the uprising had brought chaos to the Highlands. Noble Jacobite families were dispossessed of their estates, and eminent men were exiled or executed. The ordinary people were harried and persecuted, and the whole clan system, with an ancient way of life, lay in ruins.

What was being acknowledged and saluted in that little ceremony at Loch Nan Uamh, was the simple, unswerving loyalty, devotion and selfless courage of the Highland people; the ordinary folk who had sustained the hunted prince during a five-month journey through the Highlands and islands of western Scotland, with the English redcoats in hot pursuit, and a huge, unclaimed price on his head.

The flight which ended at Loch Nan Uamh, had begun at Drummossie Moor, near Culloden, and that is where my own journey would begin, as I set off to follow in the footsteps of Bonnie Prince Charlie.

HOW IT BEGAN

THE POWER struggles for the Scottish and English thrones have been sordid and brutal, but dramatic and romantic too, and it's the drama and romance which most people associate with the ancient house of Stuart. The royal Stuarts give the lie to the saying that no one loves a loser, for although the dynasty lasted for around 400 years, their history is a catalogue of disasters. Nonetheless, the family continues to fascinate historian and romantic alike, and has given us, among others, immortal folk heroes like Mary Queen of Scots, and Bonnie Prince Charlie.

The line began in 1371 with King Robert II, who was the son of Marjory, daughter of Robert the Bruce. Marjory's husband was Walter, who served the Bruce as Steward of Scotland. The office became the name, and was gradually changed to Stewart, but it was under the influence of Mary Queen of Scots that the name took the French form of Stuart. Neither Robert II nor his son Robert III made a great deal of impression on a Scotland where anarchy was pretty much the disorder of the day, and it was only with the arrival of James I (King from 1406 but a prisoner in England until 1424) that things began to change. James was known as the poet king, but he was no limp-wristed aesthete, and quickly embarked on a determined and muscular campaign to knock Scottish society into some kind of order. He played no favourites, and ultimately irritated his nobility so much that they nobly organised his murder at Perth in 1437.

The Stuart luck held good for James II who was born with a huge birthmark which earned him the name of Fiery Face. His embarrassment was cut short by an exploding cannon. It was, of course, one of his own cannon. James III had much better fortune. He was killed by an enemy at the battle of Sauchieburn in 1488. At the battle, but not in it; for the story goes that after fleeing the field and taking refuge, he was stabbed to death by a person or persons unknown. The theory is that, like James I, he was disposed of by his own nobility, who did not appreciate his style of kingship. Every Scot knows that James IV died very gallantly at Flodden Field in 1513, as did his son and about 10000 other Scots: equally gallantly, one supposes. On that day, a great part of the Scottish nobility was wiped out.

The Flooers o' the Forest, the splendid song of the battle of Flodden

Field, was long believed to have been composed at the time of the disaster, but James Hogg suspected, and Walter Scott proved, that it was of much later origin. It is a mid-eighteenth-century piece composed by the daughter of the then Lord Chief Justice of Scotland. The song is based on an earlier one by Mrs Patrick Cockburn, and these two ladies between them have given us one of the finest laments in the Scottish repertory.

The Flooers o' the Forest

I've heard them liltin' at oor ewe milkin',
Lassies a-liltin' before dawn o' day;
Noo there's a moanin' on ilka green loanin',
The flooers o' the forest are a' wede away.

At buchts in the mornin', nae blythe lads are scornin',
Lassies are lanely, and dowie, and wae;
Nae daffin', nae gabbin', but sighin' and sabbin',
Ilk yin lifts her leglin, and hies her away.

In har'st at the shearin', nae youths noo are jeerin',
The bandsters are runkled, and lyart, and grey;
At fair or at preachin', nae wooin', nae fleechin',
The flooers o' the forest are a' wede away.

At e'en in the gloamin', nae swankies are roamin',
'Bout stacks, 'mang the lassies, at bogle tae play;
But each yin sits dreary, lamentin' her dearie,
The flooers o' the forest are a' wede away.

Dool and wae for the order sent oor lads tae the border,
The English, for ance, by guile won the day;
The flooers o' the forest, that fought aye the foremost,
The prime o' oor land noo lie cauld in the clay.

We'll hear nae mair liltin' at oor ewe milkin',
Women and bairns are dowie and wae;
Sighin' and moanin' on ilka green loanin',
The flooers o' the forest are a' wede away.

THE GABERLUNZIE MAN
AND THE TRAGIC ENIGMA

Ere ye go through Scotland you shall see many good-like
men and women, and other commodities that will be to
your contentment.
(James V in a letter to his wife, Mary of Guise)

JAMES V, who was a mere child when brought to the throne in 1513,
is known to folk-singers as the gaberlunzie man. The song of the
gaberlunzie man is believed to have been written by the king.
Whether or not that is true, it describes what seems to have been a
regular royal ploy. As the 'poor man's king', James travelled the
country in a variety of disguises, and under various pseudonyms. He
took considerable risks, and chanced some very rough company; to
what ends no one seems quite sure. He is said to have been genuinely
concerned to learn how ordinary people lived, and to understand their
problems, but his stravaigings provided opportunity for numerous
encounters of a houghmagandie nature. James V broke with the Stuart
tradition by dying in his bed (in 1542), although he was only about
thirty years old when he did it. He was one of the most colourful of the
colourful Stuarts, although he has never caught the imagination in quite
the same way as Charles Edward – Bonnie Prince Charlie – or his own
ill-starred daughter, Mary Queen of Scots. He was devastated by the
birth of a daughter, rather than the hoped-for male heir, and his
much-quoted deathbed line, 'It cam' wi' a lass, and it'll gang wi' a lass',
referred to Marjory, mother of Robert II, the first Stuart king, and his
premonition that the independence of the Scottish crown would end
with his daughter Mary.

The Gaberlunzie Man

A beggar a beggar cam ower yon lea,
He was beggin' alms for charity;
And wi' mony 'Guid e'ens' and 'Guid days' tae me,
'Wad ye lodge a beggar man?' laddie wi' my tow-roo-ay.

The nicht was cauld, and the carle was wat,
And doon beside the ingle he sat,

Then he did dance and she did clap,
And aye he ranted and sang, laddie wi' my tow-roo-ay.

Between the twa, they've made a plot,
Tae rise a wee afore the cock;
And slyly then they shot the lock,
And awa tae the bent they ran, laddie wi' my tow-roo-ay.

The servant gaed where the daughter lay,
But the sheets were cauld and she was away;
And straight tae the guidwife she did say,
'She's awa wi' the beggar man,' laddie wi' my tow-roo-ay.

'Oh, gar ye ride, aye, and gar ye rin,
And haste ye find them baith again;
For she's be burnt, and he's be slain,
The gaberlunzie man,' laddie wi' my tow-roo-ay.

Meantime far oot ayont yon lea,
Fu' snug in a glen whaur nane could see,
The twa wi' kindly sport and glee,
Cut frae a new cheese a whang, laddie wi' my tow-roo-ay.

The preivin' was guid, it pleased them baith,
To lo'e her for aye, he gied his aith;
Quo' she, 'Tae leave ye I'd be laith,
My winsome beggar man,' laddie wi' my tow-roo-ay.

'My dear,' quo' he, 'ye're ower young,
An' ye hinna got the cant o' the beggin' tongue;
Tae follow me frae toon tae toon,
And carry the beggar's pyock,' laddie wi' my tow-roo-ay.

'I'll bow my back and I'll bend my knee,
I'll pit a black patch ower my e'e;
An' a beggar a beggar they'll tak me tae be,
An' awa wi' you I'll gang,' laddie wi' my tow-roo-ay.

It's three lang years have been and gane,
The beggar man cam' back again;
Back tae the guidwife a' alane,
'Wad ye lodge a beggar man?' laddie wi' my tow-roo-ay.

'O then guidwife, what wad ye give
For ae sicht o' your daughter alive?'
'It's you, fause loon, that's been the knave,
O gin I had thee slain,' laddie wi' my tow-roo-ay.

'Yonder she comes untae your bower,
Wi' silks and satins and mony's the flower':
And the auld wife cries, 'Guid luck tae the hour
That she followed the beggar man,' laddie wi' my tow-roo-ay.

The lady cam' ridin' ower the strand,
Wi' fower and twenty at her command;
The brawest lass in a' the land,
An' she followed the beggar man, laddie wi' my tow-roo-ay.

Mary Queen of Scots vied with the Young Pretender, Charles Edward, as the most glamorous and colourful of the Stuarts. She was hated and feared as intensely as she was adored. John Knox wasn't too keen; making it quite clear that he believed she had no right to be a ruler, a Catholic, or a woman. Even serious historians differ in interpretation of her character and motives, and the high drama and drastic misjudgements of her calamitous career have made her the stuff of legend. The throne passed from James V to Mary when she was only one week old, and machinations immediately began, to use her to reinstate Catholicism and nullify the Reformation established by Knox, who remained throughout Mary's life her implacable enemy. For her own safety, the infant queen was taken to France, her mother's native land, and the throne left in the care of a regent. Her childhood and formative years were spent in France, and those early influences were to have a beneficial cultural effect on her Scottish court, but also to provide reasons for suspicion and distrust. France and Spain, at odds with the Protestant Tudors, recognised Mary as Queen of England as well as Scotland, and, with her marriage to the Dauphin, who succeeded his father in 1559, she became Queen of France. Her husband died after only two years of marriage, and Mary came to Scotland at the age of eighteen.

Mary soon made clear her determination to overthrow the Reformation and re-establish the Roman Church in Scotland. Her lack of diplomacy caused much confusion and consternation, which were exacerbated by an ostentatiously Roman Catholic marriage to Henry, Lord Darnley, at Stirling in 1565. The ceremony was stage-managed by her Italian secretary, David Rizzio, a devious charmer much favoured by the queen. Rizzio was very unpopular with the court, being seen as an outsider who was alternately cringing and self-assertive, as it suited his purposes. He strongly encouraged Mary's ambitions for the Catholic Church in Scotland, and the more firmly he established himself as the queen's confidant, the more hated and feared he became. Ultimately, it was the monarch's heedless indulgence of Rizzio which was to lead to his terrible end.

Mary had quickly become disenchanted with her husband Darnley, and Rizzio further endangered his position by siding with her against him. Darnley's dislike of Rizzio deepened to obsessive hatred and jealousy, and he suspected that the relationship between the queen and her secretary had become intimate. There is no evidence for this, but Darnley went even further, believing that the child the queen was carrying was not his, but Rizzio's. Darnley's plot with some of the nobility for the removal of Rizzio, was to be part of a greater plan to replace Mary and restore the Protestant influence at court. Queen Elizabeth of England, though not directly involved, seems to have known of the stratagem and done nothing to interfere or inform Mary of what was planned. Moreover, within the plot was a subplot by the nobles, to blame Darnley for the whole affair, should things go wrong.

On 9 March 1566, Darnley and a group of his supporters burst into the queen's chambers at Holyroodhouse where she was at supper with Rizzio and some friends. It was part of the plan that Mary should be intimidated by being forced to witness the slaughter of her favourite, and though he clung to the queen, begging her protection, he was dragged forth for George Douglas to strike the first blow with Darnley's dagger. As the stricken Rizzio fell, his murderers surrounded him, inflicting fifty-six stab wounds on his body.

Although the pregnant queen collapsed in a faint during the butchery of Rizzio, she showed considerable resolve in pursuing his killers. Some were reinstated at court, some were charged, and two were hanged, drawn and quartered and their heads displayed on spikes. Darnley himself was later murdered.

Mary is seen as the unwitting victim of her own passionate nature and religious beliefs, or as a hardened devious slut who richly deserved her ultimate cruel fate. To some she is the helpless target of the more powerful Queen Elizabeth, while others regard her simply as a rather silly woman, unfitted for the high office she held. Endless words have been written endorsing all of these views, and I leave you to make your own judgement. Her life was certainly the most turbulent of all the Stuarts, and although she bore herself with dignity and courage at Fotheringay, even her execution was a shambles which degenerated into clumsy butchery, as the axeman had to hack three times before severing her head from her body.

Mary's reign was one which saw political and sexual intrigue, treachery, religious bigotry and hatred, assassination, long imprisonment, and a brutal death on the chopping block. Her end inspired both rejoicing and sorrow. Protestant England saw her death as the removal of a constant niggling threat to its stability, while Catholic France and Spain were appalled. In Scotland, even non-Catholics were aware of the loss of Scotland's independent sovereignty, but while Scotland was outraged, Mary's son James was cautious and noncommittal.

The Lament of Mary Queen of Scots

Now blooms the lily by the bank,
The primrose down the brae,
The hawthorn's budding in the glen,
And milk white is the slae;
The meanest hind in fair Scotland,
May rove their sweets amang;
But I, the Queen o' a' Scotland,
Maun lie in prison strang.

I was the Queen o' bonnie France,
Where happy I hae been;
Fu' lightly rase I in the morn,
As blythe lay doon at e'en:
And I'm the sovereign o' Scotland,

And mony a traitor there;
Yet here I lie in foreign bands,
And never-ending care.

But as for thee, thou false woman,
My sister and my fae,
Grim vengeance yet shall whet a sword
That through thy soul shall gae.
The weeping blood in woman's breast
Was never know to thee;
Nor the balm that draps on wounds of woe,
Frae woman's pitying e'e.

My son, my son, may kinder stars
Apon thy fortune shine;
And may those pleasures guild thy reign,
That ne'er wad blink on mine.
God keep thee frae thy mother's foes,
Or turn their hearts to thee;
And where thou meet'st the mother's friend,
Remember him for me.

Robert Burns

THE WISEST FOOL

WITH THE death of Queen Elizabeth in 1603, Mary's son, James VI of Scotland, became James I of England. He was the first monarch to rule over both countries, but the predicted benefits to Scotland of this union of the crowns became more and more difficult to observe. With the removal to London of the royal court, together with its patronage of the arts, Scottish literature, music and poetry slid into decline, while the language itself ceased to be that of the educated Scot, who took on more and more of the usages of the south. The continuing confusion of identity in Scottish life and culture can be said to have begun with James, the first absentee ruler. It was James VI and I who said that Scotland could be easily ruled from London by the stroke of a pen; a concept as unpopular with most Scots now as it most certainly was then. As the flow of artistic ideas diminished, warring religious factions knocked lumps off each other with that special merciless fervour peculiar to people who never doubt their own rectitude. It was James's daughter Elizabeth who created the possibility of further trouble for the Stuarts when she married the future king of Bohemia, thus opening an alternative line of succession to the throne through the house of Hanover.

James VI and I was once described as 'the wisest fool in Christendom', but he was a formidable scholar and academic and, unlike many of his line, ended a normal lifespan in his own bed in 1625, leaving behind a dual kingdom which was in better heart than when he inherited it. He was ahead of his time in heartily condemning smoking, and very much of his time in believing in, and greatly fearing, witches. His *Daemonologie* is looked on as a timeless classic, and even today is admired by those who dabble in a little frog-boiling and broom-jetting.

A LOST HEAD, A MERRY MONARCH AND A LOST THRONE

THE RELATIVELY stable kingdom bequeathed by James to his son Charles I soon disintegrated in civil war and another disruptive period for the Stuarts. Charles was the last British monarch to have any direct link with Scotland. He was born there, and had his coronation at Holyrood; but the Scots turned against him with the national covenant, rejecting his religious ideas and embracing Presbyterianism. The covenant was signed in Edinburgh's Greyfriars Kirk, and was a carefully framed protest against the king's religious impositions, rejecting the appointment of Scottish bishops and the introduction of the English prayer book.

The resistance to the changes was universal, and the covenant was signed first by the nobility, then on consecutive days by the clergy and the ordinary people. Although few punches were pulled in the document, particularly in its anti-Catholic statements, care was taken to affirm the signatories' loyalty to the crown; but it was made clear that no changes would be tolerated which had not been discussed by parliament and the assembly. About 4000 people signed, but it appeared that the theory was that if signing one's name once was effective, signing it several times would be even more so. The king's response was minimal and his reply terse, but it was not until the reign of his son Charles II that attitudes hardened, leading to the dreadful religious persecution of the 'killing times'.

When Charles I was beheaded in 1649, the Stuart line, and indeed the monarchy, could have ended there and then, but the people became disenchanted with Cromwell's notions of a republic, and sympathies swung towards Charles II. Ironically, Charles II, in his struggle for restoration to the throne, signed the covenant which had been made against his father. It is doubtful if his alignment with the Presbyterians was anything more than a political move, but it worked, for he was crowned King of Scotland at Scone in 1651. However, Charles was disinterested in Scotland, and remained indifferent to the obscenities of the killing times. In 1660 the Restoration made him King of England as well, and he managed to retain both crowns for a further twenty-five years.

Known as the Merry Monarch, Charles delivered one of the neatest and most quotable lines attributed to any royal personage. In response to the Earl of Rochester's taunt

> God bless our good and gracious king
> Whose promise none relies on,
> Who never said a foolish thing
> Nor ever did a wise one

Charles replied, 'This is true; for my words are my own, and my actions are my ministers'.'

Charles's death in 1685 led to the accession of his brother as James VII of Scotland and II of England, and saw the beginning of the end for the royal dynasty of the Stuarts after more than 300 years. James's rule was considered to be heavy-handed and insensitive, and eventually a 'convention parliament' was formed to consider the situation. The Dutch William of Orange, through his marriage to James's daughter Mary, was laying claim to the throne, and the parliament rather preferred his apparent flexibility and reasonableness to James's autocratic arrogance. In April 1689, it was decided that James had forfeited his right to the crown, and the throne passed to William and Mary.

To everyone's surprise, James's response was to cut and run for France without further arguing his case, but, not for the last time, the French failed to come up with the support which the exiled king had expected. In that same year, John Graham of Claverhouse, Viscount Dundee, known as Bonnie Dundee, rallied support for the Stuart king, and the first of several Jacobite uprisings had begun. Dundee died in a reckless charge at the battle of Killiecrankie, and although the Jacobites prevailed on that occasion, the rising fizzled out by 1690, and support faded for the inept and unloved James.

Bonnie Dundee

To the lords of convention, 'twas Claverhouse spoke,
Ere the king's crown shall fall there are crowns to be broke.
Then each cavalier that loves honour and me,
Let him follow the bonnets o' Bonnie Dundee.

CHORUS:

Come fill up my cup, come fill up my can,
Come saddle my horses and call out my men;
Unhook the West port, and let us gae free,
For it's up wi' the bonnets o' Bonnie Dundee.

Dundee he is mounted, he rides up the street,
The bells they ring backwards, the drums they are beat,
But the provost, douce man, said, 'Just e'en let it be,
For the toon is weel rid o' that de'il o' Dundee.'

CHORUS.

There are hills beyond Pentland, and lands beyond Forth,
If there's lords in the south, there are chiefs in the north;
There are brave Duinnewassals three thousand time three,
Will cry, 'Hey for the bonnets o' Bonnie Dundee.'

CHORUS.

Then awa tae the hills, tae the lea, tae the rocks,
Ere I own a usurper, I'll crouch wi' the fox;
And tremble false Whigs in the midst o' your glee,
Ye hae no' seen the last o' me bonnets and me.

CHORUS.

THE OLD PRETENDER AND THE IDEAL PRINCE

JAMES'S SON, James Edward Stuart, the Old Pretender, was known as James VIII and III, although he never mounted a throne. He made several attempts to reinstate the Stuarts; first in 1708, and then in the uprising of 1715. By the time of the final attempt in 1719, he had lost heart, and did not even join the expedition. The Old Pretender was very conscious of the fact that he was in some danger as the last living opposition to the house of Hanover, which had taken over the English throne in 1714. He needed a wife and heir, and in 1719 he married the Polish princess, Clementina Sobieska, who bore him two sons, Charles Edward and Henry.

The firstborn son, Prince Charles Edward Louis John Sylvester Maria Casimir Stuart, was born in the Palazzo Muti in Rome in 1720. He absorbed the idea of kingship with his mother's milk; or possibly with someone else's milk, for it is not generally known how the granddaughter of a Polish king nourished her offspring. The prince's father, James Edward, had left Britain as an infant, and Charles was not to set foot there until he was twenty-six, but he grew up with the assumption that great support awaited him in Scotland and England, and indeed there was discontent and unrest, however unfocused. For those with the dream of a Stuart restoration, all hopes were on the young prince, and his early years were spent in anticipation of, and preparation for, the great event.

The prince saw his first shots fired in anger at the siege of Gaeta. He was only fourteen years old, and conducted himelf under fire with the composure demonstrated only by the very brave or extremely stupid. He made a splendid impression on the officers and men, and his elder cousin, the Duke of Liria, said, 'I wish to God, that some of the great sticklers in England against the family of the Stewarts had been eye-witnesses of this prince's resolution during the siege, and I am firmly persuaded that they would soon change their way of thinking.'

Charles as a young lad was described as 'remarkable for his dexterity, grace and bearing; a fluent reader, skilful with a gun, and on a horse, and surprisingly adept at killing birds with a crossbow'; his sports were said to 'include shooting, the tennis, shuttlecock, and he is an excellent dancer. He speaks English, French and Italian perfectly, and is the ideal prince.' Ideal prince he may or may not have been, but tennis and

Bonnie Prince Charlie as a child

shuttlecock would be as useful to him as perfect English, French and Italian, in a military campaign conducted in a country where the native language was Gaelic.

Whilst everyone was delighted with the young man's prowess and development as a sportsman, athlete and budding soldier, his education was presenting problems. The Old Pretender had learned from his father's stubborn intransigence, and was finding it politically expedient to appear more tolerant of Protestantism. He thought that a Protestant teacher would broaden Charles's outlook and, more importantly, soften resistance and win friends. Clementina, however, was resolutely Catholic, and made a point of surrounding Charles with Catholic friends and instructors. Whether this conflict of parental interests had any effect on the young prince is not known, but in later life he certainly showed more religious tolerance than was fashionable at the time. It did not, however, appear to do much for his spelling. The following extract is from a letter written to his father from Gravelines on the French coast, when he was waiting to embark for Scotland.

> The situation I am in is very particular, for nobody nose where I am or what has become of me, so that I am entirely burried as to the publick, and cant but say that it is a very

great constrent apon me, for I am obliged very often not to star out of my room for fier of some bodys noing my face. I very often think that you would laugh very hartelly if you sau me goin about with a single servant bying fish and other things and squabling for a peney more or less. I hope your majesty will be thouroughly persuaded that no constrent or trouble what soever either of minds or body will ever stope me in going on with my duty, in doing anything that I think can tend to your service and Glory.

DREAM WORLD

O F ALL the Jacobite uprisings, the campaign of 1715, led by Charles's father, the Old Prentender, had had the greatest potential for success, and it failed because of bad management and leadership, not for lack of support. King George I, the 'wee German lairdie', was heartily disliked, and the Act of Union, made in 1707, was still too close for comfort, and a source of constant humiliation and frustration to many Scots. However, by the time the Old Pretender had given up hope after the 1719 rising, and transferred his ambitions for the Stuarts to his son, Jacobitism had lost much of its thrust, and people had settled, in the main, for the relative stability of the Hanoverian reign. George I had been accepted without fuss, his son George II followed in 1727, and in Prince Charles's teenage years the Stuart name was fading, but when England entered into a war with Spain in 1739, Scottish and English Jacobites saw the situation as once again favourable to their cause.

In many ways, the Jacobite court on the continent lived in a fantasy world. Charles had never set foot in Britain, and his father, who had been raised by an Italian mother, Mary of Modena, had spent only forty-five days in Scotland during the 1715 attempt, so that both father and son were as foreign to the Scots and English as German Geordie. Nonetheless, they lived with the dream of a Stuart restoration, and the fact that they heard only from disgruntled Jacobites in Britain, combined with an unshakable belief in their own right to rule, gave them a dangerously distorted picture of their situation. Most perilous of all was the naïve conviction that King Louis XV would readily throw the might of France behind the Stuart enterprise. They were to learn that his support would be erratic and unreliable, and that the French saw the Jacobite cause as no more than a means to their own ends.

DOUBTS, DELAYS AND DEPARTURE

THE YOUNG prince's education was advanced by his much-favoured Irish tutor, Sir Thomas Sheridan, and when he made his grand tour of Italy in 1737 at the age of seventeen, he was well received, and made a very favourable impression. In 1744 Charles was a vigorous young man in the prime of his physical condition. He was dynamic, charming, relentlessly optimistic, and impatient to pursue what he saw as his destiny: the restoration of his father to the throne of Britain. His first real opportunity came with a planned invasion of England by the Marshal de Saxe and a force of about 6000 men. Real French support at last! There were extensive secret preparations, and the prince and his brother Henry set off on a hunting expedition which Charles surreptitiously abandoned; travelling first to Paris, then to the little village of Gravelines, on the French coast near Dunquerque. The venture was ill fated from the start. The English got wind of the plan, and were prepared to resist invasion, but the weather did the job

Bonnie Prince Charlie as a young man

for them. A tremendous storm blew up causing terrible havoc among the ships which had already sailed, and those still in harbour. Many ships went down with their full crews and troops, and valuable supplies were lost.

The young prince was confident that the King of France would soon offer help with a further expedition, but even when he realised that this was not to be, his enthusiasm and optimism remained unaffected. He invited the Earl Marischal, who had been with his father in the 1719 attempt, to join the venture, and when the earl declined, he threatened to go to Scotland alone. He didn't. Instead, he spent some time in Paris with a banker called Aeneas McDonald, whose brother was Donald of Kinlochmoidart.

Eventually, on the basis of the news from Scotland, and of the prince's obvious commitment, the French supplied the services of Walter Rutledge and Antoine Walsh, both tough, seasoned campaigners who had been enjoying a little piracy against the English, with the tacit encouragement and support of the French. Walsh was in command of the ship *Du Teillay* (or *Doutelle*) and Rutledge had charge of the *Elizabeth*. Two captains were also provided: Captain Durbé and Captain d'Eau (or Douaud). Both ships were armed and the *Elizabeth* carried 700 men. All preparations were carried out in great secrecy, and in early July 1745, Charles Edward sailed for Scotland. On board the *Du Teillay* with him were Colonel Francis Strickland, an English supporter of the Jacobite cause, and the banker Aeneas McDonald, now a firm friend of the prince. It was hoped that on arrival in Scotland, McDonald would be able to enlist the help of his brother, Donald of Kinlochmoidart, with his clansmen and supporters. There was Charles's tutor Sir Thomas Sheridan, an experienced soldier, but now in his seventies, and another military man, Colonel John O'Sullivan. These, with George Kelly, William Murray, Marquis of Tullibardine, and Sir John McDonald who had served with the French cavalry, made up the group who were later to be known as the Seven Men of Moidart. The actual landing at Moidart also involved Duncan Cameron, who was familiar with the coastline; Aeneas McDonald's clerk, Duncan Buchanan; the Abbé Butler; and an Italian Jacobite supporter, Michele Vezzosi.

The Young Pretender was on his way to Scotland at last, but the ships had covered not much more than a hundred miles when they encountered the *Lion*, an English man-of-war carrying sixty guns. Antoine Walsh refused to engage, despite the prince's urgings, not from cowardice, but to protect his precious passenger. The *Elizabeth*, however, closed with the English ship, but came off much the worse, Captain d'Eau being killed along with forty-five of the men. Many more were wounded, and the ship was so badly damaged that it was decided that she should return to France. The loss of the *Elizabeth* with her men and supplies was a heavy blow, but the prince rejected advice to return and await another opportunity. He insisted on proceeding, and Antoine Walsh bravely agreed to press on for Scotland.

I AM COME HOME

THE LONG ISLAND is the string of islands which includes Lewis, Harris, North Uist, Benbecula, South Uist and Barra. It is so called because, on approach from the sea, it appears to be one land mass. As the *Du Teillay* approached Barra, at the southern end of

Bonnie Prince Charlie and Antoine Walsh

the string of islands, an eagle was seen circling overhead, and the Marquis of Tullibardine pointed it out to the prince, saying, 'The king of birds is come to welcome your royal highness upon your arrival in Scotland.' This was accepted by all as a good omen, which may seem a bit daft, but it was certainly no less rational than a man landing in a country of whose language he spoke not a word, with less than a dozen helpers, and with the object of taking the crown of Britain by force. Even more incredible is the fact that he almost achieved it, as we shall see.

The appearance of an unknown vessel forced the party to move off from Barra, to a landing place on the little island of Eriskay. The date was 23 July 1745. That landing place is still known as the Prince's Strand, or, in the Gaelic, Cladach a' Phrionnsa. There is a story that, before his departure from France, Charles had gathered some seeds, and that a plant which now grows on the strand is from some of those seeds, which the prince had dropped from his pocket. True or not, it is a fact that the plant, a convolvulus, is not to be found anywhere else in the Hebrides, or, indeed, in any other part of Eriskay.

This was McDonald country, and the prince knew from messages sent to France that the McDonalds were strongly sympathetic to his cause. He was shocked, therefore, when Alexander McDonald of Bois-dale in South Uist arrived to inform him that he and several other supportive clan chieftains were alarmed that he had arrived without the promised French support. Boisdale's advice to the prince was unequi-vocal. 'Go home!' Charles's reply has become famous. 'I am come home, sir, and I will entertain no notion at all of returning to that place from whence I came, for that I am persuaded my faithful Highlanders will stand by me.' On the day after the landing at Eriskay, the *Du Teillay* made the 60-odd mile journey to Loch Nan Uamh at Arisaig on the Scottish mainland, where Charles arranged meetings with some of the most important men in the Highlands.

Once again, the young Prince Charles's instincts, his buoyant spirit and courage overcame the rational argument of mature and seasoned campaigners. Time and again, by sheer optimism and force of perso-nality he won the day. One of the most respected and powerful of the chiefs was Cameron of Lochiel who at first avoided a meeting with the prince, so convinced was he of the folly of the enterprise. He initially sent his brother, Dr Archibald Cameron, to attempt to dissuade

Charles, but when he did finally meet the prince he was told, 'In a few days, with the few friends that I have, I will erect the royal standard and proclaim to the people of Britain that Charles Stuart is come over to claim the crown of his ancestors; to win it, or perish in the attempt. Lochiel, who, my father has often told me, was our firmest friend, may stay at home, and learn from the newspapers the fate of his prince.' History tells us that Lochiel was instantly won over, and declared, 'No, I'll share the fate of my prince, and so shall every man over whom nature or fortune hath given me any power.' That power was to take many ordinary clansmen to their deaths. The hard men were now falling like ninepins under the onslaught of the royal personality and when Charles asked the younger brother of McDonald of Kinloch-moidart, 'Will you not join me?' the reply was, 'I will, I will. Though not another man in the Highlands should draw a sword, I am ready to die for you.' All this willingness to die appeared to be quite infectious, and soon many of the more reluctant chiefs had committed themselves and their clansmen to the cause. There is no doubt that Lochiel's endorsement had been crucial, and from now on support for the prince grew apace.

Some time was spent at Loch Nan Uamh, drumming up further help among the chieftains; and the *Du Teillay* was sent to Lochailort to unload supplies and weapons. Charles had decided that the ship should now return to France, and after some days at Lochailort, she came back to Loch Nan Uamh to load up with provisions for the return journey. The prince granted Antoine Walsh a knighthood for his sterling services: he was presented with a ceremonial sword and some money, and despatched with a letter of warm commendation to Charles's father. With the departure of the *Du Teillay*, the die was well and truly cast, and the prince committed to pressing on with his campaign.

John Murray of Broughton, who was to be the prince's secretary during the campaign, had kept him informed of developments in Scotland before his embarkation, and he was now making every effort to conceal the prince's presence from the government authorities, and to cover up what was going on. Nevertheless, the unusual movements of clansmen, and a general air of excitement and activity, caused some suspicion and unease, and two companies of soldiers were sent from Fort Augustus to augment the garrison at Fort William. (Scotland had been garrisoned as a result of the earlier uprisings, and it was illegal for any Highlander to carry arms.) The companies, which were commanded by a Captain Scott, were ambushed and put to flight by eleven clansmen and a piper, who caused panic by their sheer ferocity, and by the racket they made. By the time the government troops had been overtaken, the eleven had been joined by more of their fellows, and Captain Scott was wounded, while several of his men were killed. This scuffle, the first encounter of the campaign, was a much more solid omen of things to come than the eagle over Eriskay, and was the beginning of the prince's almost mystical belief in the invincibility of his Highlanders.

GLENFINNAN TO EDINBURGH

Sound the pibroch loud on high,
Frae John o' Groats tae the Isle o' Skye;
Let a' the clans their slogans cry,
Rise and follow Charlie.

CHARLES HAD decided to raise his standard at Glenfinnan on 19 August, and word was sent out to this effect, but he arrived at the head of Loch Shiel to find only 150 McDonalds. Deeply depressed, he and his party waited for about two hours before the swelling sound of approaching pipes heralded the arrival of young Lochiel with a force of between 700 and 900 clansmen. The standard was then raised; a proclamation was read in which James Edward VIII and III appointed his son as regent, and a declaration of intentions was made. Shortly afterwards, McDonnell of Keppoch came in with about 300 men, then a force of McLeods from Skye, who had ignored their chief's cautions. So it went on, and very soon Charles had well over 1000 men at his command, with every prospect of many more joining him as he set off on his venture.

As the prince was mustering his forces at Glenfinnan, General Sir John Cope was organising his opposition at Stirling. The alarm was out, the garrisons were being strengthened, and there were plans to arm those clans which were supporters of the Hanoverians. This last presented difficulties, for it was felt that once armed and financed, some of

Loch Shiel

these clans would waver; and there was also a belief that even the Campbells, the most powerful of the clans to side with German Geordie, would probably become embroiled in a private war with their traditional clan enemies; namely, almost everyone else. Cope encountered all kinds of difficulties and delays which were outside his control; but made what speed he could, for he had been informed that it was Charles Edward's intention to engage him in the Corrieyairack pass, which runs between Fort Augustus and Newtonmore.

Charles was eager to build on his early victory over Captain Scott, but Cope had changed tactic and, avoiding the Corrieyairack, had turned northwards towards Inverness. Charles decided not to pursue, and sent a detachment to capture Ruthven barracks; but they encountered a sturdy resistance from the twelve-man garrison, under the command of a tough and wily sergeant called Molloy. The clansmen were forced to retire, but took with them, as prisoner, Cluny McPherson, who later threw in his lot with the prince, providing men and provisions. McPherson was later to become invaluable.

After a brief respite at Blair Castle, the force marched on to Perth, which Charles entered in some style. He had applied some basic psychology, and donned Highland dress, albeit decorated with royal finery, and he was mounted on a steed captured from Captain Scott. Extra funds were raised from the town officials, and more chieftains joined the swelling Jacobite force. The Duke of Perth, who was later to make a gallant show at Culloden, brought a number of Drummonds and Macgregors, while the Marquis of Tullibardine enlisted men of the

Stewarts, Robertsons and Murrays. Colonel O'Sullivan, another of the Seven Men of Moidart, was appointed quartermaster, and Sir John McDonald's experience with the French cavalry made him an obvious choice, with Lord Strathallan, to look after Charles's mounted force, such as it was. The most important convert was Lord George Murray, who had been appointed deputy sheriff of Perthshire, and had assisted the Hanoverians, though not to the extent of taking up arms. Murray was to be a most significant figure in the campaign, though his previous associations brought him under the suspicion of O'Sullivan, and of the prince's secretary, Murray of Broughton. The former was possibly also jealous of the man, for Lord George Murray was an impressive individual, both physically and mentally. He became noted during the campaign for his courage, endless energy and good sense, and most historians feel that Charles should have placed more faith in him, and less in O'Sullivan.

With morale now sky-high, progress was good through Dunblane, Doune, Falkirk and Linlithgow, and at Coltbridge on the outskirts of Edinburgh the Jacobites put to flight the dragoons who were supposed to be guarding the city. The taking of Edinburgh was almost comically easy, for though the castle was secure, the city itself was most certainly not. The rout at Coltbridge had caused consternation, and though it was known that General Cope's forces were now at Dunbar, the feeling of the city's officials and among the populace was that capitulation would prevent a great deal of discomfort. While negotiations were going on between the city's representatives and the Jacobites on the outskirts of Edinburgh, Lochiel led about 1000 men to the city walls. They entered Edinburgh with no more trouble than if they had had engraved invitations. A gate at the Netherbow was opened to admit a coach, and the eager clansmen rushed in behind it, but found no one to fight. The story which characterises the whole non-event is that of a citizen taking his routine constitutional, and encountering a tartanned Highlander seated idly on a cannon. 'Surely you are not one of the troops who mounted guard here yesterday?' 'Och no,' said the vicious invader; 'they've been relieved.'

Charles made a ritual parade through the city on his way to establish himself at Holyroodhouse, and he was again shrewd enough to attire himself in impressive finery, and wore in his bonnet the white cockade which had by now become the Jacobite emblem. The cockade was derived from the little white Scottish rose which the prince had picked in the garden of Fassifern, home of the young Lochiel's brother. He was much admired, especially by the ladies, though it has been observed that throughout his life Charles Edward never seemed to respond with any great enthusiasm to the opposite sex.

The short time spent in Edinburgh was used in requisitioning supplies of equipment and arms; while the recruiting sergeants went in search of more men for the Jacobite force. The prince's main preoccupation, however, was to meet General Cope, who was known to be approaching from the east coast. He summoned his officers, and with that theatrical flair which was to serve him so well, drew his sword and announced, 'Gentlemen, I have thrown away the scabbard and with God's assistance, I don't doubt of making you a free and happy people. Master Cope shall not escape us as he did in the Highlands' (a reference to the Corrieyairack). In this, he seems to have misjudged Cope, who was a very competent professional; and as we know, he wasn't wholly accurate in his assessment of God's intentions either. Nonetheless, with officers and men in high spirits, the Jacobite army made for Prestonpans and the anticipated confrontation with General Sir John Cope.

PRESTONPANS

Cope sent a challenge frae Dunbar,
'Charlie, meet me an' ye daur,
And I'll learn you the arts o' war,
If you'll meet me in the morning.'

GENERAL COPE had avoided Charles at the Corrieyairack pass, not through cowardice, but because he knew that as he approached from Dalnacardoch, the prince would be at an advantage, as the pass would be easily held, even by a relatively small force. He had also had very exaggerated estimates of the Jacobite numbers, and quite sensibly decided to make for Inverness, where he hoped to recruit from those clans who supported the Hanoverians. He met with little success in this, and marched to Aberdeen, where he took ship and headed south. He arrived at Dunbar on 17 September 1745, and was at Prestonpans on the 20th with a force roughly equal to that of the prince; about 2500. Cope decided that he would make his stand here, and although the ground was well chosen for his purposes, many of his troops were raw and inexperienced and his cavalry officer, Colonel Gardiner, was quite unwell.

The Jacobite preparations were complicated by a lack of co-operation and consultation between O'Sullivan, the prince, and Lord George Murray. Murray, however, astutely and quickly took the high ground overlooking Cope's position, but found, to his chagrin, that an expansive marshy area lay between him and Cope's position, making the characteristic rushing advance of the Highlanders virtually impossible. Cope had disposed his forces perfectly, but the Highlanders had a stroke of luck in a local man called Anderson, who conducted them, at night, by a narrow but safe route through the marsh. Taking full advantage of the haar, a local low-lying ground mist, they were able to bring themselves within striking distance of the Hanoverian lines.

The attack was made in the early morning, and although Cope's tactics were textbook perfection, the unexpected closeness of the Highlanders, the sheer speed and savagery of the attack, and the inexperience of some of the general's troops, resulted in a rout. In a matter of minutes, all had been resolved, and to dreadful effect. Cope's men had reasonably assumed that the attack would come from the high point and across the open ground, and they completely panicked when these wild men were suddenly upon them. After firing once as they raced forward, the Highlanders abandoned their firearms and, with dirk in one hand and broadsword in the other, stabbed and hacked their way through the terrified Hanoverian troops. Cope and his officers bravely tried to rally, and the sickly Colonel Gardiner received his death wound in the attempt; but there was total disorder, and before the slashing, stabbing steel, the shouted Gaelic, and the wild sound of the war pipes, the novice troops broke and fled. Cope and his officers were forced to do likewise, surviving to deliver the news of the defeat to Berwick.

The man who wrote the song *Johnnie Cope* was a local farmer called Skirving, and although he takes an ironically humorous view of the events, Skirving was quite horrified by what he saw when he visited the battlefield some hours after the carnage. As well as the damage wrought by the claymore and the dirk, there was that done by the Macgregors, who fought with scythes mounted on 7-foot staves. These simply slashed through the limbs of men and horses, and the field was strewn with severed heads, parts of arms and legs, and even torsos which had been cleaved in two. Although Charles Edward afterwards insisted that the enemy wounded be given the same care and consideration as his own men, it was the unbridled savagery of the Highlanders at Prestonpans which was partly responsible for the atrocities later committed by Cumberland at Culloden.

Johnnie Cope

This song is quite unusual in that it was composed immediately after the events it describes. It is more conventional in the sense that, though witty and colourful, it is quite inaccurate. History shows that Sir John Cope was a perfectly able and brave officer, but we should be grateful that ballad-makers have never allowed obsession with accuracy to interfere with the telling of a good story.

> Cope sent a challenge frae Dunbar,
> 'Charlie, meet me an' ye daur,
> And I'll learn you the arts o' war,
> If you'll meet me in the morning.'

> CHORUS:
> Hey! Johnnie Cope, are ye waukin' yet,
> Or are your drums a-beating yet?
> If ye were waukin' I would wait,
> Tae gang tae the coals in the morning.

> When Charlie looked the letter apon,
> He drew his sword the scabbard from.
> 'Come follow me, my merry men,
> And we'll meet Johnnie Cope in the morning.'

> CHORUS.

> Now, Johnnie, be as guid as your word,
> Come let us try baith fire and sword;
> And dinna rin awa' like a frichted bird,
> That's chased frae its nest in the morning.

CHORUS.

When Johnnie Cope he heard o' this,
He thought it wad na be amiss
Tae hae a horse in readiness
Tae flee awa' in the morning.

CHORUS.

Fye, Johnnie, noo get up and rin,
The Highland bagpipes mak' a din;
It's best tae sleep in a hale skin,
For it will be a bloody morning.

CHORUS.

When Johnnie Cope tae Dunbar came,
They spiered at him, 'Whaur's a' your men?'
'The de'il confound me gin I ken,
For I left them a' in the morning.'

CHORUS.

Noo, Johnnie, troth, ye werena blate,
Tae come wi' the news o' yer ain defeat,
And leave your men in sic a strait,
Sae early in the morning.

CHORUS.

'In faith,' quo' Johnnie, 'I got sic flegs,
Wi' their claymores and philabegs;
If I face them again, de'il brak my legs,
Sae I wish ye a guid morning.'

CHORUS.

When Adam Skirving was challenged to a duel by a Lieutenant Smith who felt that he had been slandered in another song about Prestonpans, Skirving told the lieutenant's messenger, 'Gang awa' back and tell Mr Smith I havnae the leisure to come to Haddington; but tell him to come here and I'll tak a look o' him, and if I think I'm fit tae fecht him, I'll fecht him; and if no, I'll dae as he did. I'll rin awa'.'

OVER THE BORDER

THE EUPHORIA following the runaway success at Prestonpans was marred by growing dissent amoung Charles's officers. The powerful Lord George Murray was joined by Lord Ogilvy, who had brought a force of men from Forfar, and the two often found themselves in conflict with those who had come over from France with the prince: O'Sullivan, Sheridan and the rest. Not only that, but Murray did not hesitate to tell Charles when he thought his judgement was faulty. As an experienced commander he was entitled to do so, but the prince became petulant when challenged, and the rift between him and Lord George steadily widened. In addition, the situation in Edinburgh was becoming messy, with the Jacobites unable to take the castle, and the garrison unable to clear Charles's forces out. The ordinary people were being killed and injured in ineffectual shoot-outs, and many fled the city, carrying with them their goods and chattels.

Charles spent about six weeks in Edinburgh, and exploited his success over Cope in recruiting more support. In the mean time, three French ships arrived at Montrose with men and supplies. Duncan Forbes of Culloden was raising support in the north for King George, while some of Charles's loyal chieftains travelled north to see what they could drum up among the sympathetic clans. Several hundred Chisholms and Frazers marched to join the prince, though Simon Frazer, Lord Lovat himself, could never quite decide on which side the bread was buttered. His indecision was to cost him his life, for he was eventually executed by the Hanoverians for treason. The McDonald and McLeod chiefs on Skye declined to endorse Charles's claims, but the McKinnons brought some support from the island. The two forces were becoming polarised, and more and more chieftains and their clansmen were committing themselves one way or another. The Hanoverian officers captured at Prestonpans were civilly treated, and eventually released on condition that they would not again take up arms against the prince. Few shared Charles's romantic notions of fair play, and did exactly that, when the opportunity presented itself. They saw the debacle at Prestonpans as a humiliation, a rout of real soldiers by a mob of screaming barbarians, and they were not going to pass up any opportunity of revenge and restored dignity.

The time spent in Edinburgh taught Charles something else about his

Highlanders; namely, that they had a low boredom threshold, and that they thought nothing of deserting. This they did for a variety of reasons: to tend their crofts, to visit their families, or for any one of a number of causes which they felt to be pressing at the time. These desertions were usually temporary, and they would wander back as casually as they had wandered off.

Charles could not know that Prestonpans was to be the high point of his whole campaign. He was convinced that great support awaited him in England, and that the majority shared his view of German Geordie as no more than a hated and temporary foreign interloper. Neither was true, but, nevertheless, the prince's venture would take him deep into England, and throw the Hanoverian establishment in London into near panic. The Jacobites left Edinburgh on Sunday 9 November, and marched south in two separate columns. The Duke of Perth went by Peebles and Moffat, with the baggage and supplies, and the prince by Kelso and Jedburgh. Charles was strong, young and fit, and had no difficulty in setting a pace which won him the respect of the hardiest of clansmen.

CARLISLE TO DERBY

THE TAKING of Carlisle was as undramatic and messy as had been the fall of Edinburgh. As Charles crossed the border, there was dismay in the town, for the garrison was very weak, and the only move made by the government was to appoint a Colonel Durand to organise a defence, and this with no extra troops. O'Sullivan sent a message to the town, demanding accommodation for troops far in excess of his real numbers. This device was supposed to frighten the garrison, but brought only some cannon fire. The bombardment was delayed because the Highlanders were intermingled with local people, but even when these people had dispersed the fire was not very effective. The Jacobite troops then moved away from the town in the belief that General Wade was on his way to reinforce the garrison. This information proved to be false, and they returned to begin digging in for a siege, to the renewed alarm of the townsfolk.

Colonel Durand had petitioned Wade for assistance, but he was to be disappointed. Wade replied that the Jacobites were making for Lancashire and that Carlisle would probably be ignored. Whether he really believed this, or whether he had other reasons for avoiding Carlisle, is open to question, but his response threw both the militia and the town officials into confusion. They were ultimately divided, with the mayor and his officers recommending surrender, and Durand determined to resist. In the end it was the townsfolk who swayed the decision to capitulate. Colonel Durand gave in, and Charles appointed the Duke of Perth to move in to proclaim James king, and secure the town for the Jacobites.

There had been some disagreement about the conduct of the siege, and relations between Charles and Lord George Murray continued to deteriorate. Strickland, Murray of Broughton, and especially O'Sullivan, were all for dismissing Lord George, but the cool head of the Duke of Perth prevailed. He recognised Murray's value as a commander, and his diplomatic handling of the situation was in contrast to the prince's clumsy and insensitive treatment of the man who was probably his most valuable officer. The duke having soothed Murray's bruised feelings at having been denied the honour of being first into Carlisle, a meeting was held to discuss the next move. Of the various options, the one which most appealed to Charles was to press on for the south; and, leaving a small garrison at Carlisle, this is what they did, Lord George Murray leading the first column, and the prince heading the second at about a day's march behind.

The anticipated support among the ordinary people was not forthcoming. The Highland troops were looked on as a curiosity, but there was little reaction of any kind. The reception was rather better at Preston, but in Manchester, a recruiting sergeant called Dickson, who had got too far ahead of the main body for safety, was surrounded by a crowd which turned very nasty, forcing the sergeant to defend himself with a blunderbuss. As the Jacobites moved further into England, confidence began to wane among Charles's officers, but the prince remained committed to the idea of pressing on to the heart of Hanoverian power in London. His confidence never wavered: that support would eventually come from the English Jacobites, and from the French. This was in spite of the knowledge that General Wade was closing in with about 9000 men, and the Duke of Cumberland with a force estimated to be around 12000. Progress was rapid as far as Derby, which the prince entered with his usual flourish, flags flying and pipes at full blast.

It was time to take stock, however, and an incredulous Charles was horrified to learn that the consensus was for retreat and consolidation. It was pointed out to him that the French had failed him; that Wade and Cumberland were converging with a vastly superior force, and that another would await him at Finchley. For the first time there was almost unanimous agreement with Lord George Murray, when he suggested that it might be imprudent to advance further. Murray made a very good case, and had worked out the logistics of the retreat very carefully, being confident that the Highlanders' much faster marching pace would take them safely out of the reach of the Hanoverian forces. Charles was having none of it, and delivered an impassioned speech in which he mentioned things like justice, God, right, faith, loyalty, etc. His officers, for the first time, were immune to his passion, and when they were joined by his most intensely loyal supporters, Tullibardine and the Duke of Perth, it was clear that he had lost his first argument. His last comment on the affair was rather sulky. 'In future, I shall summon no more councils. Since I am accountable to nobody but God and my father, I shall no longer ask or accept advice!'

ROAD TO DEFEAT

O	N THE retreat, the attitude of the Highland troops and of the English people was quite different from that shown during the advance. The troops had at first believed that they had turned to face General Wade, and were spoiling for a fight, but when they realised that they were in retreat, they became surly and unruly. The reaction of the ordinary people to what they saw as a ragged army in flight, was now openly hostile, and the Highlanders reacted with increasingly bad behaviour. There were unruly crowds at Manchester, and a clumsy attempt was made on the prince's life. The Duke of Perth, who had been sent on to gather reinforcements from Lord Strathallan in Perth, ran into trouble in Kendal, when his company was set upon by an angry crowd armed with sticks and stones. At Clifton, between Kendal and Penrith, there was a confrontation with an advance party of

Cumberland's force. This, though a small affair, was to be the last battle of the campaign fought on English soil and, like Prestonpans, was to have terrible repercussions for the clansmen. The Duke of Cumberland's report of the battle said that the Highlanders, on wounding some officers, cried, 'No quarter; murder them.' True or not, it was effective propaganda, and accounted for some of the outrages committed at Drummossie Moor.

Approaching Gretna, the retreating Jacobites were faced with the crossing of the River Esk, which was flowing powerfully, and about chest deep. Two lines of cavalry positioned themselves in the water, and the footsoldiers waded in between them, clinging to them. The downstream line of horses saved anyone being washed away, and the crossing was completed without loss. On the far bank, the pipers struck up a reel whilst the men danced themselves dry.

Wi' a Hundred Pipers

This is a very well-known song with an irresistible tune, but historically is even less accurate than *Johnnie Cope*, suggesting as it does that the fording of the River Esk was a bold venture on a triumphant march into England. The crossing, though well organised and executed, took place on the sad trek northwards. In places the verses leave doggerel well behind and approach low comedy.

> Wi' a hundred pipers an' a', an' a',
> Wi' a hundred pipers an' a', an' a':
> We'll up an' we'll gie them a blaw, a blaw,
> Wi' a hundred pipers an' a', an' a'.
> Oh, it's ower the border awa', awa',
> Oh, it's ower the border awa', awa',
> We'll on an' we'll march tae Carlisle Ha',
> Wi' its yetts an' castles an' a', an' a'.

> Oh, oor sodjer lads looked braw, looked braw,
> Wi' their tartan kilts an' a', an' a';
> Wi' their bonnets an' feathers an' glittering gear,
> An' the pibroch sounding loud an' clear.
> Will they ever return tae their ain dear glen?

33

Will they ever return, oor heilan' men?
Second sicht Sandy, he looked fu' o' woe,
An' the mithers a' grat when they marched awa'.
  Wi' a hundred pipers, *etc.*

Oh, wha is foremost o' a', o' a'?
Oh, wha is foremost o' a', o' a'?
Bonnie Prince Charlie the king o' us a',
Wi' his hundred pipers an' a', an' a'.
His bonnet and feathers are waving sae high,
His prancing steed fairly seems tae fly.
The North wind plays in his curling hair,
An' the pipers play wi' an unco' flair.
  Wi' a hundred pipers, *etc.*

The Esk was swollen sae deep, sae deep,
But shouther tae shouther the brave lads keep;
Twa thoosand swam over tae English ground,
An' danced themsel's dry tae the pibroch's sound.
Dumfoonert the English they saw, they saw,
Dumfoonert they heard the blaw, the blaw,
Dumfoonert they a' ran awa', awa',
Frae the hundred pipers an' a', an' a'.
  Wi' a hundred pipers, *etc.*

THE LAST VICTORY

R ETREAT DID not come naturally to the Highlanders, and they resented their officers' decision as much as had the prince himself. Desertions increased and conduct deteriorated. At Dumfries, which was loyal to the Hanoverians, they made a very bad impression, and Charles punished the town by turning a blind eye to much of their behaviour, by taking hostages and by imposing a fine of £2000 on the council. On arriving in Glasgow, the prince established himself at Shawfield House in the Trongate, and began to exact compensation for the city's lack of support hereto. Glasgow by this time

34

was expanding, and had a comfortable merchant class who were doing rather well from the union of 1707 and were quite content with a Hanoverian king as long as the profits held up. Charles was perceived to be rocking the boat which was taking them on an easy sail to comfort and prosperity. On the way south, the prince had requested funds, but had received only £5500, which he regarded as an insultingly meagre contribution, and he was even more annoyed that the city had volunteered 700 men to the government forces.

It was only the continued good sense and restraint of gentlemen like the Duke of Perth and Cameron of Lochiel which prevented the Highlanders from looting and despoiling the city. Indeed Lochiel made such a good impression on Glasgow's officials that a tradition was established there and then that whenever the Cameron chief came to the city, he would be welcomed by a peal of bells. Nevertheless, Charles made a demand for 6000 each of coats, waistcoats, and pairs of shoes, and for 12000 shirts. At the same time, he made strenuous efforts to make a good impression. There were numerous military parades, and a grand review on Glasgow Green, and there was much wining and dining of the Glasgow dignitaries, who were subjected to powerful blasts of the famous charm. This seemed to be especially effective with the well-bred ladies of Glasgow society. Among these was Clementina Walkinshaw, with whom the prince spent much time. Indeed, there is much more evidence for a genuine liaison with Clementina than there is for the later fabled romance with Flora McDonald.

As Charles prepared to leave Glasgow, the good news was that the Duke of Perth's brother, Lord John Drummond, had landed at Montrose with a substantial body of troops and much equipment. Drummond also carried a letter from France which promised support, while the dangerous Duke of Cumberland had been withdrawn from Scotland to face an expected French invasion in the south. Less cheering was the news that the powerful anti-Jacobite Campbells had at last been armed, and were raising considerable numbers against the prince. With the extra strength of Lord John Drummond's and Lord Strathallan's troops from Perth, the prince decided to attack Stirling. As in Edinburgh, the town was easy, and the castle difficult; and while Charles was obligingly changing the position of his siege guns, in response to complaints from the townsfolk, news arrived that a Hanoverian force, which included 700 Campbells, was approaching from Edinburgh, under the command of General Hawley.

Hawley, who had been brought in to replace the elderly General Wade, had been out at Sheriffmuir against Charles's father, James Edward, and was impatient with the myth of Highland invincibility. He gave his troops explicit instructions for dealing with the Highland charge, and said of 'the manner of the Highlanders' way of fighting' that 'There is nothing so easy to resist if officers and men are not prepossess'd with the Lyes and accounts which are told of them' and 'They commonly form four deep and these Highlanders form the front of the four, the rest being arrant scum' and 'They are the most despicable enemy that are.'

General Hawley arrived at Falkirk on 16 January 1746. Such was his contempt, that he refused to believe that the Highlanders, rather than digging in or retreating, were actually advancing to attack him. He ignored several warnings, and paid the penalty at Falkirk Hill, when Lord George Murray shattered his cavalry, and his foot soldiers were sent flying by the clansmen's usual reckless charge. The battle, which lasted less than half an hour, was something of a shambles, with part of the Hanoverian force fleeing in confusion, and the rest withdrawing in perfect order. It was some time before Charles's men knew that they had won, but next day the slain were stripped of everything and were left, to be described by local people as resembling a flock of white sheep on the hill. Falkirk was to be Charles's last victory.

ROAD TO DISASTER

THE SCENE for the inexorable sequence of events which now followed, had been set at Derby, with the decision to withdraw. With hindsight, many people feel that if the prince's instincts had prevailed against his officers' logic, the course of history might have been changed. The belief is that a determined advance on London would have brought the waverers and uncommitted to his support. They were, after all, the majority, and there was no great well of affection for the Hanoverian establishment. The other possibility was that the French would have thrown their whole weight behind the venture at last, with George being deposed, and the Stuarts reinstated.

Alternatively, the Jacobites could have been trapped and crushed between the forces gathering at Finchley, and the encroaching troops of Wade and Cumberland. There is yet another view, which is that for the ordinary people it probably didn't really matter. Their lives would remain basically unchanged by the outcome of a power struggle between people who took for granted their God-given right to superiority and eminence; as they did the suffering and sacrifice of those who served them. The clansmen did not rise because of a profound understanding of, and concern for, the political and religious objectives involved. Traditionally, their loyalty was to their chieftains, and they did as they were told. Many of the clans fought on the government side; among others, these included the Campbells, Munros, Sutherlands and Mackays. A few were divided. Lady McIntosh personally recruited 500 men for the prince, though her husband was a government supporter; and the Skye McDonalds fought on both sides, as did the Gordons, McKenzies and Grants, among others. Basically, the clansmen fought and died without ever really understanding why. Most didn't even care, and one Highlander, when asked if he didn't think it was a bit daft to attempt to overthrow the king, replied: 'Na sir! I never thocht aboot it. I just aye thocht how pleasant it would be to see Donald riflin' London.' The pleasures of rifling and looting were now over, and there was nothing ahead but hardship and suffering for those who had chosen to rise and follow Charlie.

It was decided at first to march out and attack Cumberland, who was approaching Edinburgh, but this plan was abandoned by Murray and the other officers. They felt that with the siege of Stirling Castle dragging on, the men becoming restive, and desertions on the increase, it would be better to move north. There they could attempt to win some of the Highland forts, in the hope that, by the spring, the French would have delivered some real support, and Charles could wage all-out war with the requisite numbers. In the meantime the Duke of Cumberland, son of King George II, was given complete command of the Hanoverian forces in Scotland. Much was made of Cumberland at the time, but military historians are relatively unimpressed by his abilities, despite his previous successes in Flanders. His strengths were that he was tough, despite his roly-poly figure, undoubtedly brave, totally committed to his cause, and brutally simple in his methods. Those who served him well were promoted and rewarded, and those

The Duke of Cumberland

who failed him were cashiered, hanged or shot. Charles's campaign in the north was marked by occasional skirmishes with the enemy, and with his own officers. The distrust between O'Sullivan and Lord George Murray had descended to downright antagonism, while the ever-patient Duke of Perth acted as mediator and attempted to cope with the prince's sulks and petulant outbursts. Nevertheless, Fort Augustus was taken, though Fort William managed to hold out.

In the meantime, Cumberland mustered his forces at Aberdeen, and when all stores, arms and transport had been secured, he marched to Nairn where he set up camp on 14 April 1746, with a force of between 9000 and 10000 men. Charles had established himself at Culloden House, but, due to a breakdown in his supply lines, some of his men were roaming the countryside foraging for food, and his force was reduced from a possible 7000 to about 5000. The prince first set out his lines on Drummossie Moor with a marshy area protecting one flank and the River Nairn the other. Lord George Murray was concerned that they faced a large expanse of open ground, so it was decided that as the Hanoverians would be celebrating Cumberland's birthday, which was on the 15th, a night march would surprise the drink-sodden troops in their beds before dawn. This most probably would have been effective, but once again, the lack of distinctive command, or even constructive consensus, brought the plan to nothing. The lines were separated on the march, with the van setting too smart a pace for the rear to keep up. Within sound of the unsuspecting Hanoverian camp, the argument went on as to whether they should attack; but when they heard drums and sounds of activity, they accepted that the element of surprise was lost and turned back – again, with protests from the prince.

CULLODEN

Drummossie muir, Drummossie day,
A waefu' day it was to me;
For there I lost my faither dear,
My faither dear and brethren three.

ALL WAS confusion on Drummossie Moor, with hungry, ill-clad Highlanders stumbling around, exhausted by their fruit-less night march. A stinging north-east wind carried flurries of sleet and snow to add to their miseries. Their positioning now was even worse than before. They had lost the boggy ground on their flank, and the farm walls, which O'Sullivan thought would afford them some protection, were seen as a hazard by Lord George. He thought they would offer cover for the enemy and wanted to breach them here and there to give his troops a line of fire, but everything had been left too late, and the walls remained. With a desperate life-or-death struggle imminent, the clans were arguing among themselves about who should have the most prestigious battle positions; and while Charles and his officers were bickering and floundering around, Cumberland's men were steadily approaching in good order. The duke had looked over the ground from the vantage point of a huge boulder, now known as Cumberland's Stone, and it must have been obvious to him that the disposition of the Highlanders virtually cancelled out their special fighting attributes: their agility, the incredible speed of their rushing charges, and the ferocity of their hand-to-hand combat.

At the first sight of the redcoats, fatigue, cold and hunger were forgotten, and a great roar of defiance went up from the ragged clans-men. They would have rushed to the fray there and then, but were restrained by their officers. The battle began with an artillery exchange in which superior placing and heavier weaponry put the Hanoverians at an immediate advantage. The Highlanders waited impatiently for the order to advance, and watched, in growing dismay and anger, as their ranks were decimated by Cumberland's guns. Charles was waiting for the duke to attack, but the bombardment was so effective that it was maintained for the best part of half an hour. The wall which Lord George Murray had wanted to breach was now of some assistance to the Hanoverians. From behind it came devastating blasts of grapeshot which one of Charles's officers reported later as 'producing a fire so terrible that they mowed down our right wing, like as they cut down a field of corn, and swept away whole ranks'.

Lord George Murray had at last to report to the prince that he could hold his clansmen back no longer, and Charles ordered the attack. Had the charge been made earlier, before the deadly bombardment had got under way, it is feasible that, against all the odds, it could have carried the day. But now it was a shambles. Charles sent a messenger along the lines to convey the order, but he was killed by a cannon ball before he had travelled very far. In the centre, Lord George Drummond had lost control of the McIntoshes, who surged forward unbidden, followed by the McLeans and McLachlans. They immediately ran into a volley of fire which caused them to veer off and blunder into another charging group on their right, and the men became so tightly packed that they could not use their weapons effectively. They were now getting in each other's way, and unable to keep up their devastating forward pace. In the mean time, the McDonalds, still sulking at not having been given the place of battle honour on the right of the prince, stolidly withstood the bombardment, but refused to advance. Only when McDonald of Keppoch rushed forward, to his instant death, did the McDonalds move. Even then their behaviour was quite irrational, as they stopped several times in a hail of musket fire, to taunt the redcoats, in the hope of drawing them out into an open fight. A rival clan would probably have been honour-bound to respond to such a challenge, but the disciplined redcoats simply looked in wonder at these fearless crazy men, and continued to pour on their murderous fire. There was no shortage of wildly courageous headlong charges, most of which were simply suicidal. The scene was chaotic and, even among the redcoats, some of the musket fire did as much damage to the soldiers' fellows as among the clans, but the Hanoverian bayonets were at last effective against the Highlanders. The redcoats had been trained at Aberdeen, not to go for the man in front, who was protected by his targe, but to stab at the next

The Battle of Culloden

man in line, as he raised his sword arm.

The men under Lord George Murray's command, who found themselves crowded by the wall and under heavy fire from the flank, nevertheless pressed fearlessly forward. Most of the Highlanders found their muskets an encumbrance during the charge, and discarded them, often unfired. The Clan Chattan men bulldozed their way through the enemy's first line, but were then met by a withering blast which killed their commander, Colonel MacGillivray, and almost everyone else. Lochiel's Cameron men by ferocious fighting also burst through, but were faced by a group of Lowland Scots under Brigadier Sempill, who allowed them to approach almost within striking distance, then loosed a volley which felled most of them in one blast. Incredibly, the few survivors still forced themselves on over the corpses of their fellows, only to die on the redcoat bayonets. Lochiel himself had both ankles shattered by grapeshot, but was carried from the field and survived the battle. At last, as the clansmen were forced to move back, some in better order than in their advance, the Hanoverian cavalry came forward and it became obvious that all was lost.

The prince, from his command position on some rising ground, watched his Highlanders raked by cannon and musket fire; hurling themselves against redcoat lines which held firm, or screaming in frustration yards from the guns; unable to move forward but refusing to retreat, and being shot where they stood. Charles appears to have been transfixed in a state of shock; unable to believe that his invincible clansmen were being so easily butchered. Cumberland's guns were eventually trained on his position, blowing the head from the shoulders of one of his men a few yards away, and injuring the prince's horse. O'Sullivan, seeing that all was lost, ordered that the prince should be led from the field.

A graphic description of the close fighting at Culloden was left by a Hanoverian sergeant who said:

> The rebels, I must own, behaved with the greatest resolution. It was dreadful to see the enemies' swords circling in the air as they were raised from strokes, and no less to see the officers of the army, some cutting with their swords, others pushing with their spontoons, the sergeants running their halberds into the throats of the enemy, while the soldiers mutually defended each other, and each pierced the heart of his opponent, ramming their bayonets up to the socket. But still more terrible to hear the dying groans of either party.

The determination of the redcoats to show no mercy was a result of the mystique of Highland ferocity. To a man from Kent, Devon or Lincolnshire, or even from Lowland Scotland, the Highlander, with his strange garb and incomprehensible language and music, was a totally alien and barbaric creature. They remembered the ferocity demonstrated at Prestonpans and Falkirk, and the clansman was further dehumanised by deliberate propaganda to the effect that he would never show mercy to a foe. Lord George Murray had issued a battle order which contained the instruction, 'Nobody, on pain of death, to strip slain or plunder 'til the battle be over.' A copy of this order, taken from a Jacobite prisoner, had a phrase added: 'and to give no quarter to the Elector's troops on any account whatsoever'. This forgery was widely circulated, and was to have terrible consequences for the Highlanders.

Most of the surviving McDonalds attempted escape in the direction of Inverness, but were pursued and cut down, as were people along the way who had had nothing at all to do with the battle. On the field itself, many of the wounded and dying were finished off as the redcoats advanced. Those who did not die of exposure during the ensuing night, were systematically exterminated next day, as the troops roamed the battlefield with club and bayonet. As rebels, Cumberland considered that they had no right to any other treatment, but there were atrocious stories of children being butchered, women slaughtered, and their bodies obscenely treated. General Hawley revenged his humiliation at Falkirk by numerous cruelties, and when he found Charles Frazer, laird of Inverallochie, lying desperately wounded among his men, he ordered one of his officers to 'pistol the rebel dog'. To his credit, this officer, one James Wolfe, refused to do so, saying that he would rather resign his commission; but another was soon found to carry out Hawley's foul order. In the aftermath of the battle, the immediate countryside was totally ravaged. Anyone crossing the redcoats' path was killed out of hand, while homes were burned and livestock driven off.

Many of the eminent people who had thrown in their lot with the prince were to pay with their lives; being beheaded or hanged. Lord Lovat, who had never been quite sure which side it was expedient to support, lost out in the end, and was executed at the age of seventy-eight. Lochiel's brother died at Tyburn in front of a cheering crowd. Many perished in the prison hulks on the Thames, and many more were transported. Some did escape to live in exile on the continent, and some even survived to have their estates restored when Jacobitism had long ceased to be a threat. The brutal excesses following the battle were only the beginning of a sustained campaign against the whole of Gaelic culture. The government, and those who saw their bread buttered on the government side, had been seriously upset and alarmed by the rising, and the Highlands were seen as the only area which could harbour any future serious dissension. A rigorous campaign was mounted against the Gaels, in which the carrying of arms was forbidden on pain of death, as was any sort of public gathering; and even the bagpipes and the wearing of the kilt were proscribed. This was, of course, extremely galling for those clans who had sided with King George. Many people believe that these measures were indeed effective, and that the ancient Gaelic culture, if not killed, was permanently crippled. Long after Jacobitism had faded as a political force, the kilt, the pipes, and all the trappings of Highland life were reinstated as a romantic fantasy, in a kind of Celtic pantomine stage-managed by Sir Walter Scott. The Scots and everyone else have been trying to distinguish between the authentic and the spurious ever since.

ANNIVERSARY

O N 16 April 1987, on a breezy, sunny day, I stood on Drummossie Moor; the site of the only defeat of Prince Charles's campaign, and Cumberland's only victory. As I wandered around this place which had witnessed such dreadful events, I pondered all the 'ifs' in *Bliadhna Tearlach* – 'Charlie's Year'. If only he had waited for solid French support. If only he had been allowed to press on from Derby to London, where there was a run on the banks, and near panic among King George's supporters. If only he had turned to face Cumberland after Falkirk, rather than going north. If only he had forced through the dawn attack on the Hanoverian camp at Nairn, and if only he had placed more faith in Lord George Murray, and less in O'Sullivan. If, if, if.

The Culloden memorial cairn

I wondered too at the almost unbelievable courage which was demonstrated here, and even more at the dreadful barbarities. I reflected on the irony that the battle has come down through history as Culloden, rather than Drummossie Moor; for the laird of Culloden, Duncan Forbes, though a supporter of King George, was a humane man, dedicated to peace in the Highlands. He pleaded with Cumberland for more civilised treatment of the people, but was dismissed by the duke as 'Forbes, that old woman who spoke to me of pity'.

A quarter of a century after the battle, Dr Samuel Johnson, on his famous tour of the Highlands, commented on the results of the Hanoverian pogrom, with the words of the Roman historian Tacitus: 'They have created a desert and called it peace.' The trauma of Culloden and its aftermath was such that a great deal of time was to pass before any songs or poems were written on the subject, and the place itself was ignored or even shunned for a long time. Eventually, a road was taken through the area, over the graves of the clansmen, and the ground blanketed by commercial forest. Colonel Charles Cameron, a direct descendant of Lochiel who had been wounded here, told me that when he joined the National Trust for Scotland, which now owns the property, the site was still covered by forestry. That was in 1982, but the trees were clear-felled, the road diverted, and strenuous efforts made to bring the battle site back to its original appearance and layout. Discreet display boards explain the disposition of the various sections of the opposing forces, and fluttering flags dotted over the wide expanse of the moor display their colours. My own impression was that the National Trust for Scotland had done a particularly fine job here. They were dealing with the story of the last pitched battle fought on British soil, one which changed the course of Scottish history; and it would have been all too easy to have converted the battlefield to a kind of tartan theme park. There is a modern visitors' centre, but the buildings are low-lying, and contain a restaurant and an excellent bookshop, with a museum and an audio-visual display. The field itself has not been interfered with, such paths and information plaques as there are, are carefully placed, and the whole effect is quietly authentic.

A simple but imposing memorial cairn was erected in 1881 by Duncan Forbes, the tenth laird of Culloden, and later presented to the National Trust for Scotland by Hector Forbes, the thirteenth laird. Strange that such a site should have remained unmarked for so long, and that the memorial should be raised by a descendant of a famous Hanoverian supporter. The inscription reads:

THE BATTLE OF CULLODEN
was fought on this moor
16th April, 1746.
The graves of the gallant highlanders
who fought for
SCOTLAND AND PRINCE CHARLIE
are marked by the names of their clans.

The gravestones of the various clans are scattered over the moor, and legend has it that no heather will grow on them. The siting of these stones is generally accepted as authentic, as the burials were carried out, at the command of the Hanoverians, by local people who would have known the various clans.

Left: Leanach Cottage; right: The Well of the Dead

There are many interesting features on the moor, among them the Well of the Dead, where the slain Clan Chattan leader, Alexander MacGillivray, was found and identified by a local lady. The redcoats were interred in a separate location, known as the Field of the English, where the plough exposed numerous human bones over a long period. The remains of the clansmen which were disturbed by the building of the road were reinterred. The old Leanach cottage, which has survived since the time of the battle, was occupied until 1912 by Mrs Annabel Cameron, who died at the age of eighty-three. Her grandmother, who

Left: Scottish Clan Battle Society; right: The White Cockade

lived nearby, was a little girl at the time of the battle. It was in an old barn adjoining the Leanach that a group of more than thirty clansmen, some of them wounded, was discovered two days after the battle. The redcoats simply barred the barn, and the trapped and helpless men were burned to death.

The scene on the day of my visit was a bustling one, as many people had come to mark the anniversary. Most were foreign tourists who looked totally bemused, though one pleasant, middle-aged American couple, who engaged me in conversation in the restaurant, were startlingly well informed. Christian Aikman, a charming and formidably energetic little lady from the '45 Association, laid a wreath at the cairn. This is an annual ritual, and Christian and her colleagues celebrate the bravery and loyalty of the ordinary Highland people as much as the memory of the prince. Christian swears that at the correct time on the proper day, the terrible sounds of the battle can still be heard. With kilt- and bagpipe-maker Ruthen Miller stalking the moor as he played the evocative *Lament for Simon Frazer*, I could almost believe her. The Scottish Clan Battle Society added a powerful presence. George Wallace leads this group of dedicated young people, who dress in the authentic garb of the period and stage terrifyingly life-like charges, skirmishes and pitched battles, which raise money for various charities. It was obvious that some of the furthest travelled visitors, such as the Japanese, were genuinely perplexed by George and his crowd. Could this be real? No one had quite enough nerve to enquire. The other group on the moor that day was the White Cockade, whose spokesman was Mike Newcomen. These lads attire themselves in eighteenth-century Highland costume and attempt to follow the tortuous route taken by Charles Edward on his marathon escape. I was to meet Mike Newcomen again in the course of my wanderings, and just how tortuous that route really was I was soon to find out, as I set off on my own journey in the footsteps of Bonnie Prince Charlie.

THE FUGITIVE PRINCE

A CCOUNTS VARY as to the manner of the prince's departure from the field at Drummossie. There are those who say that even at the last, he was desperately attempting to rally his forces, when his horse was shot from under him. Colonel O'Sullivan reports that although the horse was not killed, it was certainly hit, and was kicking and shying; and Charles himself later described blood gushing from a wound in the animal's side. He later reported that he was 'led from the field by those about me', which matches O'Sullivan's version. Lord Elcho, who was never an admirer, says that when he tried to get the prince to rally, he refused, and was gibbering in Italian, causing Elcho to accuse him of being a coward. Elcho's account is thought to be suspect, and even at this desperate stage, the prince refused to believe that his Highlanders had been routed. Sheltering at the nearby farm of Balvraid, however, he and his companions heard the victorious roars of victory from the redcoat ranks on the field where the slaughter of the wounded and dying was already under way.

As the prince took flight, he was accompanied by a handful of supporters. O'Sullivan was there, with his fellow Irish officer, Captain O'Neill; Sir Thomas Sheridan, the prince's faithful old Irish tutor; and Lord Elcho. Also in the party was Sir Alexander McLeod, whose servant, Ned Burke from South Uist, was acting as guide. They were soon fording the River Nairn at Faillie, but when I arrived there on a sunny spring day exactly 241 years later, I found a beautiful old stone bridge over the river. There would seem to have been some vague plans

Faillie Bridge

Tordarroch House

to regroup at Fort Augustus or Ruthven, but they came to nothing, though there was still plenty of fighting spirit among the officers and men. When the prince's message went out, 'Let every man seek his safety in the best way he can', there was great despondency. Many felt that it would have been better to fight on than to accept the prospect of the inevitable dreadful reprisals in the the form of murder, looting and execution.

The prince and his companions made their way through Strathnairn and Stratherrick, calling at Tordarroch House, a beautiful old building; even now in splendid condition, and still in the hands of the Shaw family. I was made very welcome there by the present owner, John Shaw. Charles found the house empty, but in fact he was still much too close to Culloden for comfort, and there was no time for even a brief pause. The fleeing group made haste past Aberarder House, and on to Farraline and Loch Mhor. This was Frazer country and relatively safe, for although old Simon Frazer, Lord Lovat, had not come out in support of the prince, he had allowed, or perhaps persuaded, his son to do so. At Gorthleck House – at that time, Gortuleg – Charles had a meeting with Lord Lovat, who exhorted him not to lose heart; reminding him of the persistence and ultimate triumph of Robert the Bruce. Charles's Irish officers were horrified by the idea, begging him to think of nothing but saving himself, and urging him to abandon all thought of further resistance, at least for the time being. The Chevalier Johnstone later reported that Lord George Murray had regrouped at Ruthven in Badenoch, while Cluny McPherson's men, who had missed the battle at Culloden, had joined forces with Murray. Many other clans were now ready to commit themselves to avenging Culloden and the 'horrors and barbarities of the Duke of Cumberland'. It was not to be. Charles was persuaded that his priority now was a

Invergarry Castle

simple one. Survival. Gorthleck is now a very pleasant family home, and I was taken through the house and shown the first-floor window through which the prince is said to have leaped to escape his pursuers.

After food and a brief rest at Gorthleck, the group pressed on for Fort Augustus. Here, a tentative meeting with his officers had been arranged, but Keppoch had been killed, and Lochiel was temporarily crippled. Others were wounded or without horses, and no one appeared, so Charles and his party made for Loch Oich and Invergarry Castle which he reached in the early hours of 17 April. Invergarry was the home of McDonnel of Glengarry, but the place was deserted when the weary party arrived, and there was little comfort here beyond mere shelter. Ned Burke caught two salmon which gave them some sustenance before they moved on after a brief rest. The castle was later sacked and burned by the Hanoverians, and when I visited it I found a romantic but very sad ruin towering over Loch Oich. When one considers the historical and social potential of the rising of 1745, coupled with the sheer drama of the Bonnie Prince Charlie story, it is surprising to find that so many of the buildings and places associated with the events are ignored and neglected: something I was to observe over and over again, as I followed in the prince's footsteps. Invergarry Castle is slowly crumbling, with notices warning visitors to beware of falling stonework, and it does seem a pity that the building should not at least be stabilised as a ruin. From here on, the prince travelled with only O'Sullivan, Allan McDonald and Ned Burke, with whom he exchanged clothes, to confuse anyone noticing the little group of travellers.

On leaving Invergarry, the prince's little band made its way down the west side of Loch Lochy, making for Loch Arkaig, and passing Achnacarry, home of Lochiel. I called in at the big house, and was most cordially received by Sir Donald Cameron of Lochiel, the present clan chieftain, and brother of Colonel Charles whom I had met on Culloden Moor. Lochiel, a charming and quietly mannered man, shares his brother's interest in the '45, and his empathy with their famous ancestor. He spoke to me at some length about the rising, and about Achnacarry, telling me that the original building was of timber. It was burned by Cumberland's troops, and only the stone gable end remains, heavily overgrown with ivy. After the defeat of the Jacobites, the estate was forfeited, and only came back into the possession of the family in 1784. The present handsomely proportioned building was begun in 1800, and was not occupied by the family until 1830. Lochiel scorned the notion that his ancestor had been taunted into following the prince; believing him to have been far too hard-headed a character to have fallen for such a device. Much more likely that he became convinced that the promised French support was indeed forthcoming.

In the mid-eighteenth century, Cameron of Lochiel was a respected and forward-looking chieftain, much concerned with controlling inter-clan strife, and initiating long-term improvements on his estates. At the time of his departure to meet the prince at Borrodale, he was planning an avenue of beech trees going towards Fort William from Achnacarry. Before his leaving, the tiny trees were simply 'sheughed in' – roughly planted in a little ditch. Lochiel set out, never to return, for he died in

Loch Arkaig

Left: Achnacarry; right: Sir Donald Cameron of Lochiel

exile in France, and the beech trees grew where they had been left. There they still stand along the river by the big house; crowded together, but fine specimens, nonetheless. When Achnacarry was restored to the family, the laird was no longer a chieftain with all the ancient loyalties and responsibilities, but a landlord – a very different thing. After taking me inside for a look at a wonderful collection of relics of the '45, Lochiel showed me the almost completed clan museum, which, among other things, should divert people like me from importuning him on his own doorstep. During the war, Achnacarry was the training centre for the commandos whose impressive monument can be seen at Spean Bridge.

CHANGES

THE MAIN differences between Loch Arkaig today and as the prince would have seen it, are the road which runs along the shore, and the fish-cages out on the waters. I was to see more and more of these as I journeyed through the Highlands and islands. The fish farm on Loch Arkaig is a fairly modest one, and the salmon here grow to only a few inches long, before they are taken away to develop to full size in the west coast sea lochs. I was taken out to the cages to see the small fish being fed in their containers, which are basically nets slung from a floating frame. Even at this size, the fish are worth about £1 20p each, and the content of each cage is valued at around £30000 . Fish farming is the great growth industry in the Highlands and islands, and while most Scots welcome anything which stimulates the problematical Highland economy, there is concern that the explosive expansion of the industry now requires more control. In

1986 Scotland produced about 10000 tonnes of fish, and by 1990 that output is expected to rise to about 35000 tonnes.

One of the main problems of control of the developments is that local authorities have influence only on the fresh-water installations, while the sea-cages, where the fish mature, are in the care of the Crown Estate Commissioners. They have jurisdiction over the sea-bed, and only they can grant leases to the fish farmers. Decisions of the commissioners are final, and there is no right of appeal. The hefty profits of the crown estates are on the increase, and the monopoly is now being robustly challenged by local authorities who feel that they should have more say in how the industry is developed in their areas. There are plans, however, to make some sea lochs no-go areas for fish farming, a move much welcomed by the conservationists. These groups are worried among other things by the visual effect of uncontrolled fish farming. The cages themselves are not too unsightly, as they lie low in the water, though there is no doubt that, with some thought, they could be designed and coloured to harmonise more effectively with mountain and loch. Real problems arise with the onshore installations, which often appear jerry-built and ugly. Those concerned with Scottish tourism feel that if this rash of unsightly structures is allowed to spread, we may lose more from the tourists than we make from the fish. Naturalists and ecologists are worried at the attacks on creatures which the commercial fish farmer may consider vermin: the otter, the osprey, the heron, the seal; and people have already been taken to court for taking the law into their own hands to protect their profits. Other

Glen Pean

concerns are the waste food which drifts down through the cages; additives to the fish food; and chemicals used to combat infection. No one yet knows what the effect of these things will be on marine life, and especially on the wild salmon. Fish farming is undoubtedly good for the Scottish economy, but perhaps some conscientious compromise is required between the various bodies concerned, and the problems should be properly addressed while they are still manageable.

HARD GOING: GLEN PEAN TO BORRODALE

LATE ON 18 April, Charles and his companions reached the home of Donald Cameron of Glen Pean on Loch Arkaig, and here the prince had his first real night's rest. It was to be invaluable, for on the next day Cameron took him to Loch Morar by way of Glen Pean. Charles negotiated this inhospitable glen in the most atrocious conditions, and so did I. The differences were that I was clad and shod in the best of modern outdoor equipment. I was well fed, and knew that I could turn back if necessary. With the redcoats in hot pursuit, there was no such luxury for the prince. The going got so bad that it was decided to abandon the horses, and it is said that, from here on, Charles wore out a pair of leather brogues every two or three days. In conditions like those in Glen Pean, that would not be surprising. It is also believed that it was about here that Charles established the habit of sustaining himself with a bottle of brandy every day. The various people involved in his tortuous journeyings in search of an escape route to France, were to be very impressed by the young man's hard-headed resistance to alcohol, but it is likely that the drinking habits established during his flight contributed to his dissolution in later life.

The ordnance survey map shows the path leading as far as the mountain bothy, and both path and bothy are excellent. After that, Glen Pean can be a nightmare in bad weather, though it is a wildly beautiful place. The mountainous walls of the glen are very steep, and there is almost no valley floor, so that the river can rise at an astonishing rate in bad weather. When I arrived at the bothy, the stepping-stones were about 12 to 18 inches above the river surface, but by the time I had had a hot drink and a bite, the stones were covered, and quite difficult to

Above Loch Beoraid

negotiate in the crossing. The mountain bothy is a difficult and isolated situation, but after my television series, I had several letters from people who remembered it as a family home. The Campbells lived here with their five children, after being flooded out of their house on the other side of the river. Going to school involved a rough walk of four miles, and all the children worked on the croft. The hill cattle were driven on the hoof to the sales at Fort William, and the men walked back over the hill from Glenfinnan, where the train dropped them. The three Campbell boys left the glen to serve in the First World War, and never returned.

Having negotiated the boulders and mud of Glen Pean, I made a rendezvous which had been arranged at Culloden, with Mike Newcomen of the White Cockade. We met at a place called Meoble, on a huge crag offering magnificent panoramic views. The weather had cleared and, looking towards the west coast, we could just see distant Loch Morar, while far below us Loch Beoraid (the loch of the grey dog) sparkled in the sun. There are many caves in this area, and Mike took me to one below the crag, which is said to have been used by the prince. The outlook is vast, and any approaching redcoats would have been seen at a great distance. The cave is hidden by a tangle of branches and rocks, and access is gained by an easy scramble down a bottle-neck which is about 15 feet deep and just wide enough for an average person to manage. At the base of the entrance, a circular chamber opens out;

Left: The steam train at Loch Eil; right: Lochailort Inn

quite roomy, bone dry, and probably fairly comfortable for a short stay. After a drum up and a bite, Mike left to pad his way over to Borrodale, whilst I made a diversion to Lochailort. I had booked a night at the Lochailort Inn for various reasons, the main one being that it has many of the features which I consider to be essential to a Highland hotel. It's traditional, comfortably appointed without being too swish, and has a pleasant ambience of easy, unforced hospitality. The landlord, Alex Duncan, is a big affable character, with a lot of local knowledge; always ready with the stories and the drams. This is the inn which was used for the interior shots in that splendid Scottish film, *Local Hero*, and I was pleased to hear that Alex had had a good crack over the bar with Burt Lancaster, among others. I was not disappointed with my stay at Lochailort, though the demands of the social life were such that sleep was difficult to achieve. In the course of my various television series, the Scottish press has had good mileage out of the notion that I am greatly mollycoddled and cosseted. Every summit of every hill is achieved with the aid of a helicopter, and I am floated around from location to location by Range Rover and Ferrari. Not true! However, I did arive at Lochailort in some style. With the co-operation of Bob Doherty and Charlie Sinclair of Scotrail, I had arranged, for the purposes of our film, to be picked up on Loch Eil side by the West Highland Railway steam train. I dozed for a little while in the sun by the side of the track, until roused by a toot from the magnificent engine still nearly a mile away down the loch. The train squealed to a halt to allow me to climb to the footplate in a dramatic cloud of steam; much to the amazement and amusement of the tourists hanging from every window. Many of them would return to Japan or Germany or America, firmly convinced that Scottish trains habitually stopped in the middle of nowhere to pick up odd vagrants with boots and rucksacks.

After my interlude at Lochailort, I was back in the footsteps of the prince, who moved across Morar, and by way of Glen Beasdale to Borrodale in Arisaig, where he had had his first meeting with the chiefs, and the fateful encounter with Lochiel. On 20 April, Charles arrived at the home of Alexander McDonald. He was well looked after here, but his feeling of security in McDonald country was tempered by the knowledge that they were close to the open sea, and in danger from searching English ships. The prince was resolved to make for the islands where he felt there was a better chance of contacting one of the French ships which were searching for him. The French had actually delivered 40000 *louis d'or*, but Charles had been unable to collect. The treasure was buried at Loch Arkaig (or, some believe, Glen Pean) and it is thought, has never been recovered. It was while Aeneas McDonald was searching for other gold, left by the Spanish, that he made the acquaintance of an old boatman called Donald McLeod. This man was to prove invaluable to the prince, and is remembered as one of his bravest and most loyal supporters. McLeod was approached by the prince with the proposition that he should pilot him out to the islands. The old man instantly agreed, saying that he would do anything in the world for Charles; but, ironically, had the departure been delayed, the party would probably have been taken off by one of two French ships, the *Mars* or the *Bellone*, which were in Loch Nan Uamh on 30 April. Once again, the prince's timing was off, and as a result he had to face several more months of wandering and privation.

An eight-oared boat was offered by the son of Aeneas McDonald of Borrodale, and on the evening of 26 April, preparations were made for departure. The party consisted of the prince, O'Sullivan and O'Neill, Allan McDonald, and old Donald McLeod and his crew of eight, which included his son Murdoch, and Ned Burke. McLeod predicted a storm and pleaded with Charles to delay his departure, but Charles was not to be put off. His decision almost cost all of their lives, for the storm broke almost immediately and their journey was made in the most hazardous conditions. Donald McLeod realised that their only hope was to make for the open sea, for they had no lights or compass; but by good fortune, they found themselves at daybreak within sight of the Long Island. Having left Loch Nan Uamh from the very spot where Charles had made his first landing on mainland Scotland, the weary group stepped ashore at Rossinish on the island of Benbecula on the morning of 27 April.

ROSSINISH TO CORODALE:
MACHAIR, MCLEAN AND MACEACHAIN

MY OWN journey to Rossinish was a short one, in a boat
piloted by Charlie Stewart from Grimsay; and I landed on a
rocky, seaweed-slippery shore on a beautiful day of breeze
and sun, with the calls of oyster-catchers and gulls in my ears. The
prince's wanderings among the islands were lengthy and complex, and
the Jacobite historian Walter Biggar Blaikie tells us, in his definitive
Itinerary of Charles Edward Stuart, that among other places he was in
Scalpay, Stornoway, Rodil Point, Loch Maddy, Loch Uskevagh,
Corodale, the Isle of Wiay, Loch Boisdale, the island of Calvay with its
castle, back to Rossinish, and from Loch Uskevagh to Skye. His trip
from Rossinish to Stornoway, on the island of Lewis, was long and
arduous, but unproductive. After walking all day on Lewis, he arrived
on the outskirts of the town late in the evening, to find the place in an
uproar, and the people terrified of the consequences of harbouring him.
He simply had to turn back.

At the army firing range on Benbecula, I was taken by Major Mike
Morris to meet Dr Mary Elliott. The range on Benbecula was in the
charge of Brigadier Harding and, over dinner, I found that he had a

Dr Mary Elliot

Left: With John Kennedy; right: Dr Alasdair McLean

great interest in, and considerable knowledge of, the place. I was especially interested in the information that the whole range is a fabulous nature reserve, and is classified as a site of special scientific interest. The area is in the charge of Mary Elliott. Dr Elliott is young, small, cheery and energetic. She wears a daft woolly hat, and has the face of a highly intelligent pixie. The face lit up with enthusiasm as she explained the features of the machair, the area between land and sea where the sand dunes are consolidated by marram grass, gradually building up a soil system. Where the sand meets the peat, the environment subtly changes, as do the types of creatures which live in it. The whole area is rich in plants and loud with the cries of dunlin, ringed plover, lapwing, redshank and sandpiper. Mary Elliott is quite obviously in her element here, and she has a particular interest in cowpats; especially the rather older ones. She is a study in concentration and anticipation, as she meticulously dissects them in search of what she rather unscientifically refers to as the 'creepie crawlies' which enjoy this type of habitat. In early summer, the machair is a wonderful sight, carpeted in flowers as far as the eye can see; and in the warmth of the sun, with the sound of foraging insects, and the skylark overhead, there can be few places anywhere in the world more captivating. I also made a point of visiting the nature reserve at Loch Druidibeg, with its ponies and geese. Otters are seen here, and eagles, and there is a fine hide overlooking the loch. The most remarkable feature, however, is a sizeable plantation of mixed trees, in an area where trees are something of a rarity. The wood was planted by Lady Gordon Cathcart, and very fine it looks too. I was introduced to another delightful aspect of South Uist by John Kennedy who runs the trout fishing on the various lochs, for South Uist estates. John has written a book called *70 Lochs: Trout Fishing on South Uist*. He really knows his stuff, but was rather unsuccessful in transferring any of his knowledge to me. We did, however, spend a very pleasant evening in one of John's boats; eventually drifting into a dramatically lurid sunset, in a silence intensified, rather than broken, by the rasping of a distant corncrake.

It was on South Uist that I met Dr Alasdair McLean, who for many years was the doctor on the island. I took to Dr McLean immediately: a short stocky man who would look like a retired welterweight boxer, were it not for his expression of benign intelligence. Talent and intelligence are a commonplace in the McLean family. One of Alasdair's brothers was the eminent folklorist Calum McLean who did such valuable work for the school of Scottish studies, John was a translator of the Greek classics into Gaelic, and the third is the Gaelic poet, Sorley McLean. Dr McLean is generally regarded as an authority on the prince's wanderings on the islands. He gave freely of his time and I found his expertise most helpful, especially on the subject of Neill MacEachain. Alasdair has written a book on MacEachain which makes it quite clear that he was much more important than the legendary Flora McDonald in the prince's escape. Dr McLean was keen to show me a place called Corodale on South Uist, where Charles Edward had had one of his few periods of real rest and relaxation in the course of his terrible journeyings. The glen at Corodale lies on the eastern side of South Uist, but while the prince and his party approached it on foot, Alasdair had arranged for us to go by sea.

At Lochboisdale, Alasdair introduced me to Archie McLellan, skipper of the *Anne Marie* which was to take us up the coast to Corodale. We set off in fine sunny conditions, and Alasdair was soon able to point out the little island of Calvay with its ruined castle where the prince had sheltered, until forced to move on by the appearance of the British ships *Baltimore* and *Raven* in the loch. There were seals basking all along the rocky shore, and through the glasses I detected a nest of young buzzards on a low cliff. At Corodale, we went ashore in a dinghy, with the assistance of Archie's helper, Cailean. Alasdair's idea was to take me up to the cave where MacEachain had hidden the prince whilst he scouted around to make sure that all was safe. Only after we had been trudging

Lochboisdale

uphill for half an hour or so did Dr McLean reveal that his last visit here had been made twenty-seven years previously. He took me unerringly to the exact spot. He told me that though some people claimed that the prince had occupied this little cave, his own belief was that Neill MacEachain had left the prince here while making sure of his welcome at the house further down the hill. There is a much larger cave which is clearly visible high on the cliff face on the other side of the glen, and legend has it that it was here that the great drinking competition took place between Charles Edward and Alexander McDonald of Boisdale. This, too, happened at the house. Dr McLean reports in his book that MacEachain closely observed the prince during the respite at Corodale,

61

Corodale

and remarked on his violent swings between quite unrealistic optimism, and fits of equally unrealistic gloom and bad temper. Neill also noted, 'with some awe', the prince's seemingly infinite capacity for strong drink. During a three-day booze up, Charles appeared to be unaffected, and is reported to have looked after his comatose companions; wrapping them in their plaids, and singing the *De Profundis* over them. One Hugh McDonald, who was present, said that although Boisdale himself was 'as able a bowlsman as any in Scotland', the prince drank him under the table.

Glen Corodale is protected by two long ridges which the Gaels call the north and south legs, or *Teach an Truibhais*, the crutch of the trousers. With the open sea in front it was a safe refuge, and the prince spent his time talking over the campaign, hunting, and drinking. He spent about three weeks here, and was given a set of Highland clothes, upon which he said, 'I only want the itch to be a complete Highlander.' What he did have, and for a considerable time, was what was then known as the 'bloody flux'; dysentery. He deduced that milk was the cause, and reverted to water, with good results. After my television series was shown, I had a long letter and printed article from Mr Albert S. Petrie of Milngavie. Mr Petrie does research into allergies, and is convinced that the prince correctly diagnosed and treated his own condition. Eventually even Corodale was becoming unsafe, with Skye militiamen searching Barra and approaching South Uist. Charles was on the move again.

Skye Boat Song

CHORUS:
Speed bonnie boat like a bird on the wing,
'Onward' the sailors cry;
Carry the lad that's born to be king
Over the sea to Skye.

Loud the winds howl, loud the waves roar,
Thunderclaps rend the air;
Baffled our foes stand by the shore,
Follow they will not dare.

CHORUS.

Though the waves leap, soft shall ye sleep,
Ocean's a royal bed.
Rocked in the deep, Flora will keep
Watch by your weary head.

CHORUS.

Many's the lad fought on that day
Well the claymore could wield,
When the night came silently lay
Dead on Culloden's field.

CHORUS.

Burned are our homes, exile and death
Scatter the loyal men;
Yet, ere the sword cool in the sheath,
Charlie will come again.

CHORUS.

OVER THE SEA TO SKYE

BEFORE LEAVING South Uist, I was taken by Alasdair McLean to Howbeg, where I met sixteen-year-old Iain MacEachain, who took me to see Neill MacEachain's birthplace. Young Iain is quietly proud of his courageous and resourceful ancestor, and agreed with me that it was pitiful to see his house as a rickle of stones overgrown with nettles. I found Flora McDonald's birthplace at Milton in a similar condition, and again I wondered at how we neglect our Scottish history.

Things were now getting very hot for the prince. He had been close to capture on the little island of Calvay, and Hugh McDonald of Armadale, Flora's stepfather, was hunting him in South Uist with a company of McDonald militia. Some of the Skye McDonalds and McLeods had thrown in their lot with the government, but, like many others, Hugh McDonald's loyalties were divided, and it was he, with MacEachain, who devised a plan to get Charles out of immediate danger and away to Skye. Alasdair McLean's researches proved to him that although the movements of hunters and hunted appear to have been quite random, there was a skilfully orchestrated programme of disinformation, which on several occasions sent the government ships off on wild goose chases. The situation was still desperately dangerous, however, and when it was known that a party under General Campbell was only two miles away, the prince retreated to Loch Uskevagh. It

Iain MacEachain

The prince's first meeting with Flora McDonald

was from here that the famous trip was made, over the sea to Skye.

Flora McDonald's stepfather was an officer in the militia, but it was he who provided the official passes for Flora's journey, the pretext being that South Uist was becoming too dangerous. Before embarking, Charles took his leave of O'Sullivan, who despite the criticisms of his judgement in the early part of the campaign, had staunchly shared all of the prince's hardships since Culloden, as had Edward Burke. O'Sullivan, Burke and O'Neill made their escape, but the doggedly faithful Malcolm McLeod, who had piloted Charles Edward over from Loch Nan Uamh to Rossinish, was later taken by Campbell's militia. Campbell was genuinely puzzled that Captain Malcolm had not simply turned the prince in for the reward of £30 000 (over a million in today's terms). When questioned, the old man replied, '£30 000! Though I had gotten it, I could not have enjoyed it eighty-four hours. Conscience would have gotten up on me. That money could not have kept it down. And 'tho I could have gotten all Scotland and England for my pains, I would not have allowed a hair of his body to be touched if I could help it.' There is no doubting old Malcolm McLeod's shining sincerity and rock-steady loyalty, but it is certain that anyone claiming that reward would not have lived long in the Highlands.

Hugh McDonald of Armadale's escape plan, which has become part of the folklore of the '45, was that Charles should be dressed in female attire and presented as Betty Burke, Flora McDonald's Irish maid. As well as the passes, Hugh McDonald had provided Flora with a letter to his wife in Armadale which read:

65

Monkstadt

My dear Marion,
   I have sent your daughter from this country lest she be in any way frightened by the troops lying here. She has got one Betty Burke, an Irish girl, who, as she tells me, is a good spinster. If her spinning pleases, you can keep her until she spins all your lint; or if you have any wool to spin, you may employ her. I have sent Neill MacEachain along with your daughter, and Betty Burke to take care of them.
      I am, your dutiful husband,
         Hugh McDonald, 22 June, 1746.

On 28 June 1746, Prince Charles Edward Stuart embarked for Skye, dressed in a calico gown over a quilted petticoat, and wearing a very becoming frilly bonnet. His companions were Flora, Neill MacEachain, John McDonald, Alexander McDonald, and two boatmen.

   They soon ran into rough weather, and the prince regaled them with songs to keep up their spirits. The best remembered of these is *The King Shall Enjoy His Own Again*, an old song even then. Early on 29 June they passed Vaternish Point on the extreme north-west of the island, and sailed across Loch Snizort to land just north of Kilbride at a place still known as Prince Charlie's Point. The plan was to go to Monkstadt, the home of Sir Alexander McDonald. Flora and MacEachain went on ahead, but found to their horror that the place was full of militia men. By good fortune, McDonald of Kingsburgh was also visiting Monkstadt. He made his excuses to leave and, arranging to meet Charles nearby, took him to his own house at Kingsburgh, with the idea of conducting him on to Portree. When I visited Monkstadt, I found the old house in a pretty advanced state of dilapidation, and

66

obviously quite neglected. Alasdair McLean took me to Kingsburgh House, where, he told me, the prince had a comfortable and jolly evening. Once again the bottle went round, and Charles slept late, throwing Flora into a frenzy of anxiety that he would be apprehended. Government troops later spread the rumour that Flora had spent the night with Charles at Kingsburgh; a silly story which Kingsburgh's wife indignantly denied. Young Allan McDonald didn't believe it either. He married Flora in 1750. They emigrated to North Carolina in 1774, but returned during the American revolution. Flora is buried at Kilmuir in her native Skye, beneath an imposing monument. When Charles said goodbye to Flora McDonald in Portree, it was for ever.

Flora McDonald's grave

She was arrested on her way home, and taken to London. By this time, however, it was obvious that the Jacobite threat was over. The undoubtedly dramatic and romantic story of her part in the prince's escape had become well known, and Flora became a popular heroine. Her prison cell became a place of pilgrimage, and she found herself the darling of London society. Her association with Charles Edward had lasted not much more than a week.

RAASAY AND CALUM'S ROAD

O N 1 JULY, Prince Charles crossed over to the Isle of Raasay on the east coast of Skye. His guide on this occasion was young Captain Malcolm McLeod, nephew of the chief, McLeod of Raasay. McLeod was known to be totally loyal to the prince, but Charles had walked into a hornet's nest, for this very loyalty had brought down the full wrath of the Hanoverians upon the island. During the period of Charles's wanderings, the campaign of fire and sword against anyone suspected of complicity with the Jacobites, had been gathering momentum. All over the Highlands and islands, people were being arrested or killed. Homes were being put to the torch, livestock driven off, and whole glens laid waste. Raasay suffered very badly. McLeod's home was looted and destroyed; there were many individual instances of rape and torture; and by the time Charles left Scotland in September, Raasay had been totally devastated.

Calum McLeod

Calum's road

Raasay is beautiful: a long strip of an island lying along a line almost exactly south to north. Charles travelled less than half its length, turning back at a place called Glame. I arrived at this point on a bright day with high clouds sailing over the shoreline of Skye; but I was heading further north to Arnish, where I had arranged to meet a man called Calum McLeod. At the approach to his croft, I was warmly greeted by Calum, a smallish wiry man with a habit of straightening himself up and pulling back his shoulders. This probably went back to his uniformed days. Between 1966 and 1976, he was a lighthouse keeper on the little island of Rona to the north of Raasay. Like many Highland people I've met, Calum hid a battery of lights under a bushel of quiet courtesy. This wee grey-stubbled man in a faded boiler suit, a ragged bunnet on his head and an old dog at his heel, won a gold medal in a Gaelic essay competition set by the Celtic Society of New York. He was a young man then, but he has been writing informed articles ever since about the traditional life of the islands.

Even more remarkable is the story of the road. The narrow road which snakes up through Raasay used to go only as far as the ruined Brochel Castle, a couple of miles short of the tiny crofting community at Arnish. One by one the people moved out, but Calum continued to petition the local council to supply a road. He was paying rates and couldn't really manage the croft without access. His pleas fell on deaf ears. He decided that he would build his own road. He set to in 1966, and by 1976 he had worn out two wheelbarrows, six picks and six shovels, as well as five hammers and five spades: but he had a road. Six years later, a horde of council workmen arrived to widen and tarmac what is now known all over the islands as Calum's Road.

Calum and his wife made me easily welcome in their house. I heartily enjoyed their company, and I was later very shocked and saddened to hear that Calum had died suddenly, only weeks after my visit. He was proud that he was descended on his mother's side from Captain Malcolm McLeod, the prince's boatman, and he told me that when Flora McDonald was released after the amnesty, it was Malcolm who had conducted her home. When Boswell and Johnson came to Raasay, to the rebuilt home of the McLeod chief at Clachan, Captain Malcolm rowed them across the Minch, as he had rowed Charles Edward Stuart twenty-five years earlier. As he rowed, he entertained them with the song, *Tha Tighinn Fodham Eiridh*, known in English as *Rise and Follow Charlie*, but more closely translating from the Gaelic as 'I Am of a Mind to Rise and Follow.'

Tha Tighinn Fodham Eiridh

Sound the pibroch loud on high,
Frae John o' Groats tae the Isle o' Skye;
Let a' the clans their slogans cry,
Rise and follow Charlie.

CHORUS:
Tha tighinn fodham fodham fodham,
Tha tighinn fodham fodham fodham,
Tha tighinn fodham fodham fodham,
Rise and follow Charlie.

On dark Culloden's field of gore,
Hark, hark, they shout 'Claymore, claymore.'
They bravely fight, what can they more?
They fight for royal Charlie.

CHORUS.

No more we'll see such deeds again,
Deserted is each Highland glen;
And lonely cairns rise o'er the men
Who fought and died for Charlie.

CHORUS.

And who shall say they died in vain,
Who fell apon that bloody plain;
For Scotland's sons shall rise again,
Who fought and died for Charlie.

CHORUS.

SKYE TO KNOYDART

The ancient proprietors of the soil shall give place to strange merchant proprietors, and the whole highlands will become one huge deer forest; the whole country will be so utterly desolated and depopulated that the crow of a cock shall not be heard north of Druim Uachdair; the people will emigrate to islands now unknown, but which shall yet be discovered in the boundless oceans, after which the deer and other animals in the huge wilderness shall be exterminated, drowned by horrid black rains. The people will then return and take undisturbed possession of the lands of their ancestors. (Kenneth McKenzie, *The Brahan Seer*, in the seventeenth century)

EVERY MINUTE on Raasay put the prince in terrible danger, and he left secretly on the evening of 2 July. This was another fearsome journey, with the waves lashing over the gunwales, the oarsmen pulling frantically, McLeod bailing, and everyone pleading vainly with the prince to turn back. They eventually landed on Skye at a place called Nicolson's Rock, in Trotternish. Charles's idea was to make contact with McKinnon of Strathaird.

Captain Malcolm, who wished to make the journey by sea, was

Sligachan, Skye

persuaded to conduct the prince overland, though it involved a journey of about twenty miles through dreadful, punishing country. Charles travelled on this occasion as Malcolm McLeod's servant, using the name of Lewie Caw. Before finally leaving Skye, from a beautiful place called Elgol (then Elligol or Elliguil), the prince is said to have thanked McKinnon for his help and hospitality, by presenting him with the secret recipe for Drambuie. Another legend? Who knows? But if it's true, anyone who has enjoyed this lovely golden liqueur after a good meal, has reason to be grateful that the recipe didn't escape with the prince.

Before leaving Skye, Charles Edward said his final farewells to the stalwart Captain Malcolm McLeod, who had earned his total respect. The prince presented Malcolm with some money and a silver buckle and then, with four oarsmen plus John McKinnon and the Laird of McKinnon, set out for mainland Scotland. They were on the south shore of Loch Nevis by the next morning, and after two or three days, made their way up the coast. Charles had another narrow escape here, for he was pursued by a group of militiamen who had observed his boat from the shore. His escape was only made possible by the strength and skill of his Highland oarsmen who simply outpaced the opposition, and forced them to give up. Charles's party wandered this mountainous area for some time, and always in great danger. By the time of their arrival, the redcoats had established a line of camps which ran between Loch Eil and the head of Loch Hourn. These camps were only about half a mile apart, and effectively cut off the approach to the sea across the whole area of South Morar, North Morar and Knoydart. From the mountain known as Druim Chosaidh, on the fringe of Knoydart, they could see the line of fires which barred their passage, and when they did creep through them under cover of darkness, they were so close that they could hear the conversation of the sentries. It was in this wild country too, that Charles narrowly escaped death. He missed his footing while crossing a little burn on a cliff face, and only the speed and strength of McDonald of Armadale and Donald Cameron saved his life.

I decided that I'd like to take a closer look at Knoydart, and to this end I went to Mallaig and boarded the *Western Isles*, which is owned and skippered by Bruce Watt. I joined Bruce in the wheel house, and he told me that he used to be a herring fisherman, but took over the 65-foot *Western Isles* from his father, who, in his time, had carried Eric Linklater when he was researching his book, *The Prince in the Heather*. Bruce's dad was also, at one time, the skipper of the shark-fishing boat, the *Leopard*, owned by Gavin Maxwell, who wrote his famous otter stories at Camusrory, at the head of Loch Nevis.

The journey up Loch Nevis takes about three-quarters of an hour, depending on conditions, and even in the dreich weather which I encountered, the village of Inverie looked superb, with the little white-painted buildings curving around the bay. Not so long ago this was an all-Gaelic community. Now, it's the visitors who have the Scottish accents, and the village has taken on the character of a colony of the English home counties. The local school caters for the children of incomers, though their teacher, a dedicated lady called Mary Hill, strives to give them a knowledge of, and feeling for, the local culture.

Knoydart, recognised as one of the last great wilderness areas in

Elgol, Skye

Europe, has had a chequered history, and a series of interesting owners. Among the most striking was Lord Brocket, who bought the estate in 1930. Brocket was a wealthy brewer from the Midlands of England, who looked on this huge chunk of Scotland quite simply as his personal playground. There have been, and are, popular and well-meaning lairds. Brocket certainly was not one of them. He was an open admirer of Mr Hitler, and was once a guest at his birthday party; and when Ribbentrop was in Britain seeking support among the upper classes, he was an honoured guest at Knoydart. Archie McDougall, who lived in Knoydart during Brocket's tenure, remembers that the local people had almost a prison camp existence. When the gentry were in residence, he says, 'You could not go around freely. Local children were not allowed to be seen on the beach or within vision of the mansion house. No tourists or campers were allowed on the estate, even although there did exist rights of way, access tracks through the rough bounds.' Archie told me (by letter) that when Lord Brocket bought the estate from a Mr Bolsby, 'a highly respected gentleman', it was one of the best-maintained areas in the north. Brocket, however, was interested only in sport, and all else was neglected. During the war, Knoydart was requisitioned as a training area, but very soon after the end of hostilities, people found themselves being made redundant, and forced to leave, to be replaced by labour from outside. Archie McDougall and several other ex-servicemen found themselves victims, and, with perfectly good land being allowed to go to waste, they decided to take action. The local priest, Father MacPherson, composed a letter to the Department of Agriculture, who got as far as doing a survey of the area.

Bruce Watt

Mallaig

Thereafter, the affair stagnated, until Archie and six others moved on to the land and laid claim to it in 1948. Similar desperate measures had been effective in the past, and in retrospect Archie feels that had they stuck to their guns, and even gone to prison, they would ultimately have won. In the event, they lost. The ensuing publicity showed Brocket in such a bad light that he sold up not long afterwards, but not before clearing out almost all the original people of the area. At the time of writing, Archie McDougall and Duncan McPhail are the only two surviving members of those who became famous as the Seven Men of Knoydart.

In more recent years, there was a tremendous outcry when it was rumoured that Knoydart was to be purchased by the Ministry of Defence, but that never happened. The present owner, who bought the estate with a now departed partner, is English property developer Philip Rhodes. I visited Philip at Inverie House, and was greeted by a tall, good-looking and likeable urbane type, who made me very welcome, and talked with some enthusiasm about the estate. His plans and policies have taken a critical hammering in some quarters, but he makes several perfectly valid points in defence. To begin with, he is quite frank about the fact that he is a businessman who is interested in profit. He also claims that an area which was pretty well moribund is now

75

Philip Rhodes outside Inverie House

reinhabited. Buildings have been or are being restored, and several small businesses have been established. There is a sawmill run by a chap from Sheffield; a Nottingham man has the guest house and restaurant; and there is a pub and a shellfish farm. Philip Rhodes claims that he has been instrumental in establishing a community – albeit a different kind of community – here in Knoydart, and feels that he has done well by new owners and tenants. Critics see him as an asset-stripper who has sold off various packages of Knoydart to individual and group buyers from Jersey, Guernsey, Barbados, Belgium, Holland and Switzerland. He has obviously added to his loose change while still retaining 20000 acres and Inverie House, which will be used as a sporting and conference centre. It is surely unproductive to criticise people like Philip Rhodes, who is a legitimate businessman operating within the law; but perhaps more attention should be paid to a system which allows Scottish land and the lives of the people on it to be juggled around on the international property market. The system, which is unique in Europe, can only be duplicated in countries which we think of as feudal. People's homes can be bought out from under them by Danes and Arabs who look on Scottish land simply as a form of currency; and as their clients and friends are mainly interested in vast empty tracts for sporting purposes, we inevitably have a new kind of Highland clearance.

The Seven Men of Knoydart

It was down by the farm of Scottas
Lord Brocket walked one day,
When he saw a sight that troubled him
Far more than he could say.
For the seven men of Knoydart
Were doing what they'd planned,
For they'd staked their claims and were digging drains
On Brocket's private land.

'You bloody reds,' Lord Brocket yelled,
'What's this you're doing here?
It doesn't pay, as you'll hear today,
To insult an English peer.
You're only Scottish half-wits,
But I'll have you understand,
You highland swine, these hills are mine,
This is all Lord Brocket's land.'

Then up spoke the men of Knoydart,
'Away and shut your trap,
For threats from a Saxon brewer's boy
We just don't give a rap;
For we are all ex-servicemen
Who fought against the Hun.
We can tell our enemies by now,
And Brocket, you are one.'

When the noble lord he heard these words,
He turned purple in the face.
He said, 'These Scottish savages
Are Britain's black disgrace.
I know it's true, I've let some few
Thousand acres go to pot;
But each one I'd give to a London spiv
Before any bloody Scot.'

77

'You're a crowd of tartan bolshies,
But I'll soon have you licked.
I'll send to the court of sessions
For an interim interdict.
I'll write to my London lawyer
And he will understand.'
'Och, to hell with your London lawyer,
We want our Scottish land.'

Then said the men of Knoydart,
'You have no earthly right.
For this is the land of Scotland,
And not the Isle of Wight.
You may scream and yell, Lord Brocket:
You may rave and stamp and shout
But the lamp we've lit in Knoydart
Will never now go out.'

A WET WALK, GLEN AFFRIC
AND THE SEVEN MEN OF GLENMORISTON

L EAVING INVERIE, I set off for Mam Barrisdale and the Gleann an
Dubh Lochain (the glen of the little black loch). This was the
wettest walk of my whole trip, surpassing even the Corrieyairack Pass in its exposure; though it started off well enough, as I passed
Lord Brocket's monument. The memorial stands like a giant beehive
on a prominent hillock dominating the entrance to the glen, and is, I
think, suitably ugly. Passing the Dubh Lochan, I sheltered and had a hot
drink in some old buildings which were part of a defunct fish-farming
venture of more than twenty years ago. The broken remains of the old
cages still lie in the loch, something which people fear may happen
again, if the present entrepreneurs find any reason to abandon their
projects. From the loch, the path steadily steepened to the summit at
1500 feet. Not terribly high, but I had come up from sea level, and it
was a steady, head-down, rather miserable plod in nil visibility, and on
a path like a stream. After a night at Barrisdale bothy, where my gear

would have dried out if the last person to bed hadn't let the fire go out, it was on to Kinlochourn. The day was in total contrast to the one on Mam Barrisdale. Birds sang, the sun shone, the colours were vibrant after the rain, and the waters of Loch Hourn danced and sparkled – around the fish cages. These two days were probably my worst and best of the whole outing. Loch Hourn is indescribably beautiful, and the path wanders along, sometimes down close to the shore, and sometimes climbing steeply above the waters, and offering quite breathtaking views.

At this stage, Charles Edward made for Glen Shiel, Loch Cluanie, Glen Affric, Strathglass and Strathfarrar, which brought him to the most northerly point in his wanderings, on Ben Acharain. Glen Affric is said to be the most beautiful glen in Scotland. Many glens are said to be the most beautiful in Scotland, but Glen Affric must surely be a genuine contender for the title. It's a sad, desolate kind of beauty, however, and when I spoke to Duncan McLennan, who has lived and worked here all his life, he told me that the last family, apart from his own, left the glen in 1947. Duncan and his wife live in a beautiful little house in an idyllic situation, though the isolation must sometimes cause problems, but Duncan told me that the glen, which used to ring with bird calls, is now silent. He remembers a little field near his house, which was the nesting place of snipe, peewit, curlew, and even greenshank, quite a rare bird. They are all gone, and Duncan blames the pine marten. Now a protected species, the pine marten, is a strikingly handsome animal, but a ferocious and highly successful predator, with no real natural enemies in the wild. Duncan is sad about the loss of the glen's bird life, and actually witnessed a pine marten destroying the last black-throated diver's nest in the area. The beauties and wildness of Glen Affric have been exploited by the film companies, and *Kidnapped*, and *The Last of the Mohicans* were filmed here.

It was while Prince Charles was in the hills above Ceannacroc that he came upon the cave of the famous Seven Men of Glenmoriston. I was keen to see the cave, and I knew the very man who could take me to it; but firstly I made a little detour to the monument of a man called Roderick McKenzie. The roadside cairn is at Ceannacroc, on the Glenmoriston-Glenshiel road. Roderick McKenzie was a young man who is said to have closely resembled the prince in height and physique, as well as in colouring and facial appearance. McKenzie was surrounded

With Duncan McLennan

and attacked by a gang of redcoats, and as he received the death blows, he cried, 'Oh villains, you have killed your prince.' The jubilant redcoats cut off the head of their victim, and carried it back to Fort Augustus, giving Charles something of a breathing space until the deception was discovered. McKenzie's grave, which bears a simple wooden cross marked *R.M. 1746*, is on the opposite side of the road from the cairn.

My next stop was at Tomchrasky, where I was met at the door by a very noisy and aggressive Jack Russell terrior, which would have been a truly terrifying animal were it not for the fact that it was about 3½ inches high. Its owner, Tom Girvan, is as big and quiet as his dog is wee and noisy. Tom's family owns Tomchrasky and the Ceannacroc estate, and he took me the ten miles or so up the glen to the cave. The famous hiding-place is in a jumble of great rocks, and is really a huge stone which has split in three, creating a large area with a sloping roof and three entrances. The cave in Coire Doe was used by Donald and Hugh Chisholm, Hugh McMillan, John McDonald, Alexander McDonald,

Gregor Macgregor, and Patrick Grant who owned what is now Tom Girvan's home. These were extraordinary people. Glenmoriston had been subjected to the full wrath and venom of the Hanoverian policies of total extirpation of anything and everything even remotely connected with the Jacobites. The whole glen had suffered fire and sword. Every inhabitant had been killed or hunted out, and all livestock had been driven off. The seven men, rather then being cowed by the superior forces ranged against them, had resolved to fight a relentless guerrilla war against their oppressors, and were determined to continue to the death. Tom Girvan showed me the place where the prince had made his bed, as well as the little stream mentioned in Alexander McDonald's account, which still flows inside the cave.

It was from here that Charles, accompanied by the seven, headed off to the northernmost point of his journey. He had come this far in the belief that there was a ship at Poolewe, but this information proved to be false, so he turned south to retrace his steps all the way back to Loch Arkaig, where he found that Lochiel had fled and that Achnacarry had been put to the torch. The prince was in the Loch Arkaig area for about ten days before travelling by Loch Lochy and Loch Oich to the Corrieyairack Pass, and over to Ben Alder by way of Creag Meagaidh.

I decided to do the same and wished I hadn't.

Roderick McKenzie's memorial cairn

THROUGH THE WINDOW TO CREAG
MEAGAIDH AND BEN ALDER

THE HIGH parts of the Corrieyairack Pass are very exposed, and, with my usual luck, I slogged up it on a very wet and blustery day; but it was only when I crossed over to Creag Meagaidh that I faced the full force of the weather. The Creag Meagaidh nature reserve rises up from Loch Laggan to a crescent of cliffs at the top of Coire Ardair. These huge walls, towering over a little lochan, are scarred by huge gullies and buttresses, and rise to 3700 feet. At one point, this vast escarpment is cleft by a strange V-shaped fissure, which is known as the window. The prince is believed to have come through here, and so did I. As I came over the ridge, I looked down a steep slope strewn with gigantic tumbled boulders, some as big as houses, and the wind gusting up through the gully nearly lifted me off my feet. To add to the fun, I had a mixture of stinging hail, sleet and snow in my face. All very exhilarating, though not quite what one expects in August. But the squall passed, and the prospect down through the reserve to Loch Laggan was well worth all the discomfort.

As I lost height, there was more shelter, and the terrain changed from bare broken rock to a sturdy growth of trees of various kinds, and it was here that I met Dick Balharry. Dick is the chief warden of the Nature Conservancy Council for the north-east of Scotland, and a man much respected for his knowledge of and commitment to wildlife and conservation. I had spoken to Dick on my radio programme on a couple of occasions, but it was good to meet him on his own territory. He told me that the Nature Conservancy Council was especially keen to gain control of this estate when it came on to the market in 1983. When I wondered if the buying price of £430000 of public money was perhaps a bit daft, Dick explained that the area is really special. Rising, as it does, all the way from the shores of Loch Laggan to the crags and cliffs at nearly 4000 feet, it provides habitat for everything from ducks, divers, and woodland birds, to merlin, eagle, peregrine, ptarmigan and dotterel. There is also some very old natural woodland which Dick and his colleagues will maintain and develop by controlling grazing by deer; and, of course, the ground supports most of the Scottish mammals, including the pine marten and the wild cat. Dick Balharry is convinced that when the prince passed this way, there were many more trees, and

The Coire Ardair 'window'

much more game and other wildlife; but his idea is not to reproduce the past, but to develop the nature reserve to the maximum of its natural potential.

Prince Charles is believed to have stayed at Aberarder House, which is now part of the Nature Conservancy Council's property, and when he left here, he crossed Loch Laggan into Badenoch and made his way to Ben Alder. He met with Lochiel again at this point, and the meeting has been described as a joyful and emotional one. Lochiel, who, in the early stages, had warned the prince against his rash venture, who had

The cave on Ben Alder

been crippled at Culloden, whose home had been burned, and who was now hunted and in desperate straits, still expressed his devotion and loyalty to the prince. He would have knelt at his feet, but Charles prevented this, fearing that they would be observed from the surrounding hills. Charles remained with Lochiel for two days, and was then taken by Cluny McPherson to another hiding-place which was described as 'very bad and smokie'.

I approached Ben Alder from the Loch Pattack side and had permission to stay at Culra Hunting-Lodge. It was here that I met Mike Thomson and three of his friends, all of them successful businessmen in the whisky trade. Mike and his group follow in the footsteps of the prince, but do it the hard way, wearing the *filli mhor* – the big wraparound kilt – and other clothes of the period. They sleep out, and live on oatmeal, plus any fish or animals they are able to catch. That night's accommodation at Culra Lodge, though pretty basic, must have seemed quite luxurious to them. The food was plentiful, there was a sufficiency of drams, and the songs and stories went on well into the night. I had invited an old friend along on the Ben Alder section of the walk: the Scottish cartoonist, Malky McCormick. Malky is a keen outdoor man, and as well as singing a few songs, he kept us entertained by furiously caricaturing everything and everyone in sight, and with devilish accuracy.

Next morning, Malky and I awoke to find Mike Thomson and friends long gone, so we packed up and made our way along the shoulder of Ben Alder to a spot overlooking Loch Ericht and the old Ben Alder cottage, reputed to be haunted. A couple of hundred feet above the loch is another fine cave where Charles spent several days. The famous 'Cluny's Cage', which has been much written about, is generally agreed to be higher up on Ben Alder. Donald McPherson said, ''Twas situate in the face of a very rough, high, rocky mountain which is still a part of Ben Alder, full of great stones and crevices, and some scattered wood interspersed.' The cave was constituted of boughs and rope woven into an existing growth of holly, and two separate floors were constructed to accommodate six or seven people. The writer Affleck Gray believes that the site of Cluny's Cage is indeed high up on the face of Ben Alder, and this is endorsed by Tom Weir, certainly one of our most knowledgeable outdoor men. The cave I visited is given on the ordnance survey map as 'Cluny's Cage', but though the tumble of boulders and the huge flat stone which forms its roof would make it wind- and water-tight, it does seem to be too close to Loch Ericht and the possibility of a boat suddenly appearing around the headland, to be really safe. Charles stayed at his strange refuge between 2 and 13 September, but Cluny McPherson is said to have remained concealed here for nine years before escaping to France, where he died after only a year.

INTO LEGEND

C HARLES FELT as safe and secure at Ben Alder as he had been at
Corodale in South Uist, but when a messenger arrived on 13
September to say that there were French ships seeking him on
the west coast, he and his companions left immediately. They went by
Glen Spean and Glen Roy and crossed the River Lochy, to spend the
night of 16 September at the ruined home of Lochiel, by Loch Arkaig.
In the meantime, government ships were scouring the east coast,
possibly directed there by more deliberate misinformation. On 19
September, the prince's party arrived at Loch Nan Uamh to find two
French ships awaiting them. Charles was taken on board *Le Conti* and
transferred to *L'Heureux*, with Lochiel and his brother, Dr Cameron,
while Cluny McPherson left to make his way back to Ben Alder. In the
very early hours of 20 September 1746, Prince Charles Edward Stuart
sailed out of Loch Nan Uamh, out of Scotland, and into legend.

Bonnie Prince Charlie leaving for France

During his campaign, the prince's undoubted courage and resolve had sometimes been blemished by fits of wilfulness and petulance which were worrying and unattractive. As a fugitive in hourly danger of his life, dirty, hungry and weary, and plagued by lice, dysentery and midges, he was unfailingly courageous, cheerful and resilient, and well deserving of the incredible loyalty and self-sacrifice of his Highland supporters. His venture was a failure, and the next forty-two years of gradual disintegration and dissipation are perhaps best forgotten. It was those five hunted months in the hills and glens which have made Bonnie Prince Charlie the great Scottish folk hero of song and story.

The prince's monument, Glenfinnan

Hamish Moore – *Lochaber No More*

The Last of the Stuarts

The last of the Stuarts is sunk in the grave,
And their name and their lineage is gone;
And the land of the stranger a resting place gave
To him that was heir to a throne.
But the noon of their glory was soon overspread,
And their sun he grew dark with dismay;
And the clouds of misfortune hung over their head,
Till their sceptre had vanished away.

No more for their cause shall the trumpet be blown,
Nor their followers crowd to the field;
Their hopes were all wrecked when Culloden was won,
And the fate of their destiny sealed.
Cold, cold is that heart which could stand o'er his grave,
Nor think of his fate with a sigh;
That the glory of kings, like a wreck from the wave,
Here lone and deserted must lie.